COUNSELLING
OLDER PEOPLE WITH
ALCOHOL PROBLEMS

of related interest

Counselling the Person Beyond the Alcohol Problem
Richard Bryant-Jefferies
ISBN 978 1 84310 002 7

Person-Centred Counselling for People with Dementia
Making Sense of Self
Danuta Lipinska
Foreword by Brian Thorne
ISBN 978 1 84310 978 5

Cognitive Behavioural Therapy with Older People
Interventions for Those With and Without Dementia
Ian Andrew James
ISBN 978 1 84905 100 2

COUNSELLING OLDER PEOPLE WITH ALCOHOL PROBLEMS

MIKE FOX AND LESLEY WILSON

FOREWORD BY DR MARTIN BLANCHARD

Jessica Kingsley *Publishers*
London and Philadelphia

CONTENTS

Dr Pamela Griffiths, psychotherapist, lecturer and author, is Mike's inspirational and supremely gifted supervisor. For most of the last decade she has acted as the most supportive guide and mentor, and her experience and wisdom have contributed substantially to the development and effectiveness of the practice described here. Words are insufficient to express our gratitude.

We offer grateful thanks to Dr Lindsey Nicholls, Lecturer in Occupational Therapy, Aneurin Owen, former Director of The Institute of Alcohol Studies and Dr Filippo Passetti, Consultant in Substance Misuse Psychiatry, who all kindly took time to write in support of the need for this book, and also gave generous further encouragement.

We would like to thank Dr Marsha Morgan, Reader in Medicine and Honorary Consultant Physician at the Centre for Hepatology at the Royal Free Hospital, for consistent support and encouragement, as well as a valuable introduction at a time when we were seeking a publisher. We would also like to thank her colleague, Chris Miller, Senior Specialist Alcohol Nurse at the Centre for Hepatology, for most helpful advice regarding medical aspects of detoxification.

We wish to thank Sue Benson, editor of the *Journal of Dementia Care*, for generously allowing us to use a substantial part of an article published in the journal as the basis for Chapter 12, 'Dementia and Alcohol'.

We are very grateful to Helen Murphy, Administrator at the Institute of Alcohol Studies, for directing us towards several research papers that have informed the text; also to Dr Claudia Cooper, Consultant in Old Age Psychiatry at the Royal Free Hospital, for answering questions regarding the effects of alcohol on the diagnosis and treatment of dementia and for providing her research paper examining the relationship between alcohol and cognitive impairment in older people.

All of the following colleagues and friends have offered help in writing this book through advice, suggestions, encouragement, enlightening conversations or shared experience in practice: Anna Betz, Angela Byers, Ruth Cooke, Anna Derham, Melanie Dixon, Moya Forsythe, Dr Elina Galis, Lali Gostich, Bancroft Grant, Kate Hancock, Kay Johnson, Gary Jones, Mary Longley, Alice McKenzie, Jamie McNulty, Gillian Oliver, David Richards, Monica Riveros, Silvana Tharratt, Rachel Turner and Alison Warren. We offer them all our sincere thanks.

FOREWORD

This book is important for our society if it wishes to be fair, just and caring. It is important for primary care, social care, mental health teams, alcohol teams and the many other organisations that try to care for our older people. But above all it is important for older people with alcohol problems – a group that can be invisible, unless we allow ourselves to see them and their distress. It is a testament to them and demonstrates the work that can be done to bring solace even where situations appear to be desperate.

I first met Mike Fox when he attended our community mental health referrals meetings. His presence was greatly valued especially when all the age-related problems many people encounter, be they physical, mental or social, had suddenly become even more complicated with the word 'alcohol' being read out. It was reassuring to know that we had with us a worker with particular skills and experience, who would be able to give that older person a real opportunity for change and who would sensitively try to engage them, finding the time and space in which to explore their issues from their perspective, being with them in the ups and downs of the relationship, helping them with their decisions, and supporting them through their choices.

Times, however, are changing. A recent Department of Health document entitled 'A report on the development of a Mental Health Currency Model' appeared in April 2008 reflecting changes that have occurred elsewhere in the NHS where specific surgical or medical conditions can be 'costed' and efficiency targets brought in. The paper claims to want to put the 'service user' at the heart of the NHS through explicit patient choice and to do this by the development of Payment alcohol – and the many other reasons for 'not helping' that are always close to the surface when times are economically challenging, this book documents a way that older people with alcohol problems can and should be offered help.

Dr Martin Blanchard
Consultant and Senior Lecturer in Old Age Psychiatry

PREFACE

In this book we aim to offer a practical and philosophical perspective on an important and specialised area of counselling that has thus far received little attention. We offer our own experience and, most importantly, that of Mike's clients, whose stories herein illustrate both the purpose and methods of the approach we describe.

Between us we have worked with older people in a wide variety of capacities and settings, and long before this book was conceived had each witnessed the damaging effects of alcohol dependency when working with older people in the community. Over time we have developed a profound interest in the life stage issues and cultural implications of working with an older client group who we believe have different specific needs from those of younger people. We also believe that these can be met most effectively by specialist services and interventions. This is particularly so in the field of alcohol misuse, where generic provision is rarely designed to cater for the requirements of older problematic drinkers.

Older people who develop alcohol problems are a far more varied group than might be imagined. Hence the counselling work described here has proved to contain many fascinating aspects, not least the opportunity to witness rich and diverse life experience, highly personalised philosophies of living, as well as some very individual and even idiosyncratic ways of being in this world involving much suffering but also much humour. The approach outlined in this book has evolved in response to this varied and often very personal need. It is broadly person centred in orientation but also contains a strong

WHAT DISTINGUISHES THIS CLIENT GROUP?

In this chapter we will describe some of the salient features that tend to distinguish older people with alcohol problems. We will also begin to describe in general terms how older people may differ from younger people in relation to the issues and backgrounds they typically bring to counselling.

Perhaps the most striking thing about this client group is their sheer variety, reflecting the many parts of society in which alcohol misuse has become an endemic factor. The service in which Mike currently works deals with clients from the age of 55 upwards, and nearly 40 years separates the youngest clients from the oldest. In addition clients come from a wide range of social, educational and professional backgrounds, as well as from a variety of cultural and ethnic origins, some of which might not be readily associated with the use of alcohol. What then are the collective factors that make these people different?

There is greater variation in the duration or span of drinking problems than with a younger client group, and also more potential for variations in patterns of drinking and triggers for drinking. In addition older people generally, and particularly those with alcohol problems, are more prone to risk of social isolation. There is also more risk of the drink problem being masked by other conditions associated with old age, such as memory loss and confusion (particularly for those with dementia), unsteady gait and reduced mobility, poor co-ordination, falls, and depression or mood swings. Thus recognition of problematic drinking can be delayed by our expectations of what is

WHERE TO BEGIN? ALCOHOL AND IDENTITY

Am I an 'Alcoholic'?

'When I've stopped drinking for two years I'll give myself the present of calling myself a teetotaller.'

In this chapter we will discuss the relationship between self-description and identity in the context of alcohol misuse. We will explore how identifications made in early life can influence the development of an alcohol dependency. We will also describe how the counsellor's attitude towards the client can facilitate a new or less restricted sense of self.

The language we choose to employ in relation to alcohol and to people who are experiencing alcohol-related difficulties is crucial. For many people with an alcohol problem the term 'alcoholic' represents a primary statement of identity. Historically clients accessing support or treatment have been encouraged to use this term, and failing to describe oneself in this way would be viewed as denial. It is not uncommon to encounter former drinkers who continue to call themselves alcoholics long after alcohol has ceased to be a dominant factor in their lives, and whose difficulties with alcohol encompassed a relatively minor proportion of their life as a whole. They may do this for various reasons. Such an epithet might serve as a reminder of the need for vigilance. Some people believe that their physiological through which development can take place to be, the more opportunity there is for an individual to become self-aware and gain ability to make choices; two precursors of freedom from what has come before. If we believe that our character is substantially formed within the first few years of life, change in later life can seem an unlikely prospect, and such an attitude can represent a significant impediment to successfully overcoming dependency. Conversely the belief that development can be lifelong by its very nature engenders a more fluid sense of possibility, and one that can counteract the feeling of stuckness and inertia so prevalent in this client group.

No one working with an older client group can fail to acknowledge the power of early conditioning; however, we believe it is unnecessarily limiting to regard it as the sole determinant of all subsequent behaviour and experience. Clearly the present self results from all that has gone before. The experiences occurring at all stages of life and the narratives of many of the clients Mike has worked with validate the impact of events that have happened to them at various stages of adulthood. This point is of particular significance in relation to clients whose problems with alcohol began late or comparatively late, and especially to those who were previously able to drink moderately.

It might surprise some older clients, particularly those with an addiction, to realise that they are seen as having potential, as being capable of change, or simply as being able to 'have a life'. Self-esteem is invariably low at the outset, and often motivation also. People with addictions have often incurred opprobrium and adverse judgement, and have learned to view themselves harshly, or feel beyond hope, or as not deserving of help. Furthermore the very idea of change can be threatening to those with an addiction, whose personal habits in relation to alcohol have often developed their own homeostasis. For these and doubtless other reasons we have found this client group to be particularly sensitive to the view in which they are held, and likely to value an attitude and philosophy in the counsellor which is positive and enabling of change. They may also assimilate such an attitude and make it their own, an invaluable step in challenging the dominance of addiction.

Josh came to see me at the recommendation of a psychotherapist whom he was seeing as a private client. Prior to this he had had other fruitful experiences of counselling or psychotherapy, but had yet to address successfully his longstanding problem with alcohol, which stretched over nearly 35 years. At the time we met, Josh was 61 and had tried to stop drinking 'thousands of times'. He presented as a thoughtful, somewhat cerebral man who spoke openly in a measured and considered way. He was seeing his other therapist regarding 'issues relating to intimacy' and wished to see me concurrently to address his drinking. I was willing to proceed with this arrangement providing it created no confusion or conflict: alcohol counsellors frequently work with clients who are simultaneously receiving other psychotherapeutic or psychiatric help. Josh was clearly mature in his approach to therapy, and in the event no difficulty transpired.

Josh was born in London of a Jewish mother of Eastern European extraction and an English father, whose parents were a Welsh Gypsy father and a Scottish Presbyterian mother (when asked how he would describe his ethnicity Josh, possibly considering the question intrusive or inappropriate, replied rather dismissively 'celtic slav'). He described his mother as 'intellectually ambitious' and his father as 'warm but distant'. His mother died when he was ten, and henceforth, in the aftermath of her death, his father began to raise him according to Jewish customs and tradition, where previously this had not been the case. During the next few years, despite failing his 11 plus exam, Josh began to flourish academically.

Josh's description of his father, who was illiterate, was intriguing. A self-contained, detached man whose behaviour was normally 'very controlled', he was able to 'sense the need to be quiet'. To illustrate this Josh explained that his father would sometimes sit in silence for a period of hours in the evening and on the following day present him with a large sum of money with no explanation as to its source. As a teenager Josh had admired this ability to 'turn thought into money', finding the idea romantic, although it later became apparent that his father was involved in criminal activity. Josh felt that he had inherited some of this resourcefulness in that he could make money when he needed to, albeit by more legitimate means: he was a highly accomplished data analyst with advanced computer skills.

Henceforth we met fortnightly, and after nine months he said that if he could remain abstinent for two years he would award himself the accolade of teetotaller. At this point I was approached by a journalist who had been commissioned to write an article about older people and alcohol. She wondered if any of my clients would consider being interviewed. Josh immediately came to mind and when I asked him he was willing.

The article, when published, proved a watershed for him. He had agreed to be named and photographed, and described the experience as a 'coming out'. He still had lingering doubts as to whether some of his friends understood the extent and true nature of his relationship with alcohol, and he felt that he had made a powerful statement to refute the possibility of denial or minimisation. An inherently altruistic man who derived both meaning and sense of self from helping others, his action also represented a considerable act of generosity. Paradoxically, in taking such a determined stance, he was reminded of a time when as a five-year-old he stood between his parents, 'two large people arguing', and had felt as though he did not exist.

As our work continued Josh passed through other milestones of abstinence: 300 days, a year, the first time he ceased to be aware of 'how long since I stopped drinking'. We began to meet monthly, then every three months. With characteristic self-deprecation, he said he felt that our relationship was the main factor in his success, and I was reminded again of the simple value of having one's experience witnessed.

He continued to develop, at one point contemplating writing a novel in which he would outline a plethora of possibilities for the rest of his life. He embarked on another degree and became a locum teacher of English as a foreign language. He produced a remarkable analysis of the relationship between his alcohol use and blood pressure, having first been able to reduce and then stop his medication as his readings fell. He also became a leading member of a group that was part of the service in which I worked, and produced an exquisite website to record their activities.

As our work neared its end Josh feared being alone with the depression that still troubled him. As he had ceased to see his original therapist some time previously, I was able to refer him into a local psychotherapy service, where he could continue to gain insight and support. We still speak occasionally on the phone.

3

REASONS FOR DRINKING

Alcohol and Paradox

'I didn't need any more guilt.'

In this chapter we will explore how and why alcohol problems develop, drawing primarily from client testimony and observation derived from practice. We will describe some common traits of temperament or personality that we have found to be prevalent in people with alcohol problems and explore what distinguishes problematic drinkers from 'normal' drinkers. We will look at the influence of environment and also reflect on clients' beliefs regarding the possibility of physiological or psychological predisposition. We will also explore the paradoxical reasons clients give for drinking as a way of establishing how they are trying to meet their needs through alcohol.

WHAT DISTINGUISHES THE 'PROBLEM DRINKER' FROM THE 'NORMAL DRINKER'?

It is common to meet people who drink regularly or even heavily but who appear to be able to stop at will. They clearly enjoy alcohol and perhaps drink more than is good for their health, but do not appear to be compelled to drink, or to drink immoderately, if they choose not to. This begs the question: what distinguishes people who develop an alcohol dependency from those who drink regularly yet do not? There is no definitive answer; however, we suggest that the latter rarely if ever use alcohol to meet fundamental needs. Conversely people who develop a dependency invariably drink to compensate for some sort of deficiency or lack, even if they are not aware of what this might be, or that their drinking represents a compensatory activity. While making this distinction it is also important to mention that clients' histories frequently reveal that previously moderate or relatively contained drinking has escalated into dependency during times of stress or difficulty. This profile would be typical of late onset drinkers (see Chapter 6, 'Working with Types and Patterns of Drinking'). Where this occurs it can indicate what level of stress, type of stress or timing of a stressful event/s has the effect of increasing an individual client's susceptibility. It also suggests that in some cases the distinction between normal and dependent drinking can relate to surrounding contingency.

When working from this hypothesis, that dependency stems from genuine need that is not being met, it is always valuable to encourage clients to explore their reasons for drinking, and to do this in a spirit of genuine enquiry and without cynicism. What need or needs are they trying to meet by using alcohol? How else might their needs be fulfilled?

By nature of the fact that they are entangled in an addictive behaviour these questions might take time to answer, particularly if a client is not naturally introspective and appears initially to have little self-awareness. Many people who develop an alcohol dependency seek instant gratification or immediate relief, the former suggesting an avoidance of processes involving patience or effort, the latter an inability or unwillingness to stay with pain or discomfort when alcohol or some other substance can appear to alleviate it. For these reasons amongst others, learning to explore motives involved in problem drinking, and the emotions surrounding them, can be challenging for both client and counsellor. By its nature the work involves scrutiny of areas that that hitherto the client has preferred not to consider and may have learned to hide or protect. However, this type of sensitive and concerned enquiry can help identify which personal resources the client needs to develop in order to overcome their dependency. It can also highlight which behaviours and habits could most usefully be changed or modified to enable the client to meet their needs without recourse to alcohol.

HOW ALCOHOL PROBLEMS DEVELOP

It is possible to speculate widely regarding the underlying factors that influence the development of an alcohol dependency. Three that are commonly mentioned are the relationship between temperament and alcohol dependency, the question of physiological or psychological predisposition, and the influence of psycho-social or environmental factors. We will explore each of these in turn.

Temperament and alcohol dependency

People who develop alcohol problems usually struggle to process their feelings. For some people this might represent a lifelong difficulty, for others the ability to know and express how they feel can be disrupted by an accumulation of life events which are eventually experienced as overwhelming. We believe that enabling the client to learn to recognise and process how they feel is undoubtedly the most powerful therapeutic element in overcoming alcohol dependency and in preventing relapse. As suggested above, problematic drinking is usually characterised by the attempted avoidance of difficult thoughts and emotions. We will say more about this in later chapters.

A less general but still prevalent feature among people who develop alcohol problems is that they tend to globalise their current mood, that is, to project it into the future and to allow it to colour the past. Thus a comparatively transitory mood, for instance of anxiety, depression or indeed optimism, can seem overwhelming or intractable, or even be imagined to be permanent, *while it is being experienced*. This is particularly likely in clients who experience significant mood swings, and could be described as a defining characteristic of problematic drinkers who also suffer from bipolar disorder. Such a propensity can contribute significantly to the likelihood of relapse, as a person experiencing an elevated mood may become over-confident and therefore less guarded about the possibility of relapse, while a lowered mood might seem so consuming and intractable that drink appears the only means of escape. Ironically the consumption of alcohol both exacerbates and perpetuates any tendency towards instability of mood.

Clients who experience strong fluctuating moods inevitably find it difficult to maintain a balanced perspective towards their drinking and other aspects of their lives. Therefore they can benefit greatly from any interventions that help them to develop insight and maintain a degree of objectivity. Feedback from the counsellor regarding patterns that become apparent in the client's moods and their resulting effects can be extremely valuable, as can encouraging the client to keep a mood diary that can be related to patterns of drinking or to the desire to drink. Practices that encourage the client to monitor their thoughts and feelings regularly such as mindfulness and conscious relaxation can also be very helpful, although they must be introduced with care as to the right timing. This is because, by their nature, they are likely to challenge the client to become aware of thoughts, experiences and body sensations, some of which are likely to be painful, all the more so for being suppressed by alcohol. Learning to stay with unpleasant experience, as opposed to drinking to deaden the feelings it can evoke, can make new demands upon the client's internal resources. Sometimes these practices can also bring back powerful and disturbing memories, another reason why they should be introduced carefully. Nevertheless all of these interventions can help this type of client to increase their self-awareness and objectivity towards their feelings. This will in turn enhance their ability to tolerate and process lowered mood, especially if they are able to recognise that in many cases it may be transitory or of limited duration, thereby lessening its power to trigger drinking.

High achievers are also noticeably prone to alcohol problems. Clearly there is nothing inherently wrong with high achievement; it is usually regarded as laudable, but several typical characteristics make such people vulnerable. They are often very driven and struggle to switch off, and hence more prone to use alcohol to relax. The more driven the person the more likely this is to be the case. They also tend to have very high standards and can be intolerant of fallibility in themselves and others. Additionally their inherent competitiveness can make them self-critical, yet simultaneously over-concerned with external opinion. Perhaps for these reasons they often reveal surprisingly low self-esteem, a factor that can further compound any tendency to misuse alcohol.

Experience suggests that people who are very driven by nature are quite likely to be immoderate in a variety of ways. Sometimes for such people the task of learning to stop or limit their drinking can represent a metaphor for the ability to learn limits and apply moderation in other areas of their lives. Therefore they may benefit from an exploration of whether their drive to achieve is motivated in part by fear or lack of self-acceptance, in which case it is more likely to generate discontent and hence misuse of alcohol. They may also benefit from learning to negotiate cut-off points within their various endeavours, so that they do not drive themselves to the point where they are in deficit. High achievers frequently drink to sustain effort, but also to compensate for the toll that the quest for excellence and productivity takes on their energy and wellbeing.

Physiological or psychological predisposition

This is not a medical book and it would not be appropriate here to try to delve into medical evidence regarding the probability of inherited predisposition to alcohol addiction. It is, however, interesting to note briefly what some clients say and believe about this.

It is common to hear clients with a clearly defined history of problematic drinking say 'Although I have a drink problem I'm not an alcoholic' or to ask for an opinion as to whether they actually are 'an alcoholic'. Statements and questions such as these suggest a belief in the possibility of an intrinsic predisposition to alcohol addiction. As we have already suggested, such a belief can significantly influence the client's sense of personal identity and hence the course of the work and of their capacity to effect change in relation to their drinking. Clients with a family history of problematic drinking are particularly likely to feel that their relationship with alcohol is pre-ordained, and may believe that they have inherited a psychological or physiological propensity to alcohol dependency. Whether or not this is the case, and there is no way that the counsellor can prove or disprove whether such beliefs have factual validity for a particular individual, it is very important to understand the extent of their potential impact. It is the sense of inevitability regarding their fate that distinguishes this type of drinker from late onset drinkers, or even those long term drinkers who believe that their eventual dependency stemmed originally from environmental factors.

> I liked the taste of beer, its live, white lather, its brass-bright depths, the sudden world through the wet brown walls of the glass, the tilted rush to the lips and the slow swallowing down to the lapping belly, the salt on the tongue, the foam at the corners. (Thomas 1940, p.93)

Bearing this in mind, when working with clients who have been drinking problematically for most of their lives, it can be enlightening to ask if they can remember their first experience of alcohol and, if so, to note how they describe this. The quote above is informative as it typifies a certain type of response: that of utter sensory delight. This contrasts markedly with the mild (or not so mild) initial aversion of those who feel that they had to acquire a taste for alcohol. Furthermore it is not uncommon for clients to describe an immediate sense that they metabolised alcohol differently from those around them, and that its effect was somehow more vivid, profound or compelling. Others have noted that from the outset they drank more or faster than their companions, or that they quickly developed compulsive behaviours around alcohol.

Whatever the cause of these responses they clearly indicate a more profound susceptibility and hence a more intractable attachment to alcohol. Experience suggests that clients who describe this type of relationship with alcohol are most likely to regard their dependency as inevitable, an attitude that will reinforce any current physiological or psycho-social dependency. This type of client is most unlikely to be able to learn to drink moderately, although, if abstinence proves impossible, they are sometimes able to limit their drinking to a point where harm can be minimised. They are also, at the outset, unlikely to be able to imagine the possibility of either stopping drinking or thereafter maintaining abstinence, and this can be a considerable hurdle to overcome in terms of moving the work forward. Where clients struggle to anticipate a positive outcome there is an onus on the counsellor to 'hold the hope' on behalf of the client, and anything that helps the client to demonstrate to themselves that they are able to exert some control over their drinking will be valuable.

Psycho-social/environmental factors

In Chapter 5 we will describe how the initial assessment can be used to begin to understand and clarify specific aspects of the client's relationship with alcohol, an important component of which is their history of drinking. Exploring this will help to reveal how their relationship with alcohol has evolved and what are its causal factors. Hence it is always pertinent to ask at what age the client began to drink and at what age they became aware that their drinking represented a problem, and to consider the possible impact of social and environmental factors before and during this time span. It is also especially important to explore the client's subjective perception of their influence. The following are among the most frequent examples of circumstances that older clients describe as causal or contributory:

- childhood relationship with parents, siblings and other family members

- the effect of childhood abuse

- factors within their education

- wishing as a young person to emulate role models, part of whose persona involved conspicuous drinking

- the influence of factors within their culture and/or ethnicity

- drinking as part of the culture of their work or working environment

- drinking to ease pressure at work

- current abusive relationships or abuse experienced in adulthood

- difficult relationships, breakdown of relationships or loss of relationships

- drinking as a response to illness

- retirement or redundancy

- bereavement

- social or existential isolation

- the prospect of dying.

We have tried to shape this list in terms of chronological likelihood, as far as that is possible. The factors within it could be divided into three categories in terms of their chronological relationship to individual client's history of drinking:

1. *Early experience or experience that occurred in an earlier phase of life:* It is always valuable to explore childhood and early experience where possible because of its formative potential in relation to a client's character and outlook. Events experienced early in life can sometimes also be found to be a direct cause of problematic drinking. The same can also be true of events that took place in an earlier part of adulthood. This does not necessarily mean that drinking became an immediate problem at the time the experience occurred, although this may be the case, rather that the genesis of the problematic relationship with alcohol can be traced unequivocally to this point.

2. *Experience that is currently influencing the client's relationship with alcohol:* This includes recent experience that may have triggered late onset drinking as well as current events that continue to affect a longstanding problem. For instance, significant life events such as bereavement or retirement may both mark the start of a drink problem or exacerbate an existing one. In the latter case a client may present immediate concerns regarding current experience which it may later be possible to contextualise, as more is learned about the relationship between their personal and drinking histories.

3. *Future concerns or fears:* It is very hard for young or even middle-aged people to imagine old age, perhaps in part because older people so often display stoicism in the face of the fears and uncertainties that inevitably accompany it. For instance, it is a rare person who reaches the age of 60 without experiencing at least one significant bereavement. Although age may bring both joy and benefits it is also a time of loss and greater likelihood of illness, and in the face of this it is natural to begin to consider one's own mortality. It is also a time when practicalities may take on a greater significance in the face of increasing uncertainty about the sustainability of one's physical and mental powers. The trepidation that may be felt in the face of such challenges, particularly for those who are socially isolated, can have a significant effect on a client's relationship with alcohol, whether or not it had previously been problematic. Because of this a sensitive exploration of 'hidden fears' can be very valuable, especially if it can lead to referral to other forms of support.

ALCOHOL AND PARADOX

There is often much that is contradictory in the behaviour and motivations of people who develop alcohol problems, and the way they use alcohol can sometimes exemplify this. Drink can come to serve more than one purpose, and sometimes the second purpose can appear diametrically opposed to the first. This can particularly be the case with longer term drinkers, who may with the passage of time view alcohol as a panacea for a variety of needs. While this can be confusing and perplexing for the therapist it also indicates the potential for inner conflict in people who turn to alcohol in an attempt to ease pain or solve problems. Therefore working with this client group can involve recognising and, if possible, reconciling polarised needs and motivations.

The following are examples of apparently contradictory reasons people give for using alcohol:

To create or enhance a sense of empathy	To feel less
To become calm or reduce anxiety	To celebrate
To gain social confidence	To stimulate thought/creativity
For energy	To cut off from feelings
To enhance memories	To elevate mood or find excitement
To feel more involved	To switch off from company
To experience the thrill of secrecy	For relaxation
To help to forget	To disengage emotionally
To amplify or increase feelings	To quieten the mind
To mourn or as part of grieving	To be able to speak more openly

In practice it can take time for such needs to become apparent. As already suggested, the use of alcohol is not always accompanied by self-awareness, particularly when the motivations for drinking are complex or contradictory. However, dependency is always accompanied by need, and needs can change and evolve. Furthermore when alcohol is used to meet a need it can ironically tend to submerge it, so that even if the need was conscious in the first place drinking will tend to hide or disguise it. Helping clients to become aware of their needs, without criticism or blame, is a crucial part of any work involving alcohol. Therefore, where two reasons for drinking appear to oppose one another, it can be helpful to acknowledge the validity of both, and to encourage the client to explore the possibility of learning to balance or reconcile the polarised needs they represent.

Maureen is a practising artist. She is in her mid 70s, has experienced multiple bereavements, and believes that the sense of panic she frequently experiences upon waking derives from her vivid awareness of life's impermanence. At the time of writing she and I have been meeting for 14 months and she has been abstinent for five since having a community detox. Although she no longer drinks she is a proud hostess and still serves wine to her guests when holding dinner parties. She has begun to reflect upon how her relationship with alcohol developed. In retrospect she can identify two particular influences. The first stems from her mother who was a suffragette. As an art student Maureen would drink pints of beer (in an era when this was very unusual) to demonstrate parity with her fellow students, who were mainly male. She now believes that this was a way of expressing her sense of emancipation as a woman, and also of defining herself as someone more able to exercise independence than had been possible for her parents' generation. The second influence came from her tutors, some of whom were highly cultured with considerable reputations in the art world. From them she learned a love of fine wines and international cuisine and she has come to realise that her aesthetic appreciation of wine derives strongly from these associations with glamour and the broadening of her early horizons. It is likely that her drinking remained highly contextual – always as an accompaniment to her evening meal – because of this association. It is also likely that her aesthetic appreciation of alcohol prevented her drinking from becoming more indiscriminate.

Sometimes, when a client has gained ascendency over their problem, examples of a paradoxical relationship to alcohol remain, but in a healing sense. Examples would be the client who, secure in abstinence, was able to reduce his blood pressure by imagining himself holding a glass of brandy, or the client who spent a blissfully peaceful holiday working, without temptation, in a Californian vineyard. Perhaps the greatest paradox of alcohol misuse, and one that clients often come to realise, is that they have sought release through a substance whose use has instead resulted in dependency.

4

A NON-DIRECTIVE APPROACH

Abstinence or Moderation?

'*I don't expect you to be the nursemaid of my indecisiveness.*'

In this chapter we will define what we mean by a non-directive approach. We will explore the demands that working non-directively can make upon both counsellor and client, also why we believe it is preferable to an approach that insists upon abstinence.

In the purest sense of the term a non-directive approach to counselling could be described as one in which emphasis is placed on the client to define what outcomes they desire from therapy and to work towards them without instruction, prompting or suggestion from the counsellor, whose role is that of a facilitator. Whether such purity is achievable is a matter for debate, particularly in view of the detachment it asks of the therapist. Whether it is viable to work non-directively within the field of alcohol is even more contentious, particularly as clients with alcohol dependencies are more likely to expect specialist knowledge and expertise from a counsellor (Heather and Robertson 1997).

In the context of this book we would define a non-directive approach as one in which the client is encouraged to clarify and realise their own goals in relation to alcohol. Even this can require considerable forbearance on the part of the counsellor. Working with clients whose history of drinking contains no evidence of self-control, or whose medical diagnosis suggests that alcohol will cause immediate damage, can entail a suspension of disbelief on the one hand, and restraint from the natural impulse to help by trying to impose change on the other. The counsellor might also feel concerned about the possibility of collusion in self-harm or wishful thinking. To offset this prospect, and in order to remain authentic, it is appropriate to offer the client information and feedback relating to possible outcomes of the path/s they choose, and particularly to state when a choice is likely to cause or perpetuate physical or psychological damage. This will help the client to make informed decisions regarding the course of action they pursue.

It is reasonable to ask at this point what the merits of a non-directive approach are, especially as many would insist that abstinence is the only viable goal for those with alcohol problems. The questions that we will suggest might be asked during assessment, as well as much else that will follow in this book, indicate that there are many different patterns of drinking, reasons for drinking, and reasons for wanting to change the way one drinks. The complexity that this implies highlights the range of needs one might encounter in this work, as well as the value of recognising the individual needs and motivations of each client. This requires more flexibility than a blanket insistence on abstinence, which can:

- deter clients who initially are unable to contemplate the prospect of refraining from drinking completely

- deny clients the opportunity to reach abstinence via a period of controlled drinking, which might involve staged reduction

- deny the opportunity to return to normal or moderate drinking (some late onset clients *are* able to do this)

- force the issue of detoxification prematurely

- deny the option of harm minimisation for clients who are unable to abstain.

Clients who arrive at abstinence via attempts to drink moderately often learn a great deal about their relationship with alcohol in the process. An example would be a client for whom the possibility of moderate drinking represented a metaphor for balance, who aspired to relinquish the behavioural extremes to which she was prone, and who came to realise that she used alcohol to help her both to engage and disengage in personal relationships and in the social realm generally. Thus she would drink to try to gain social confidence but also to escape from company when contact with others became too intense. This type of insight is valuable because it reveals the need behind the drinking, and so offers the opportunity to learn to meet it without alcohol.

The non-directive style of working also acknowledges that change cannot be imposed from outside and offers the possibility of self-knowledge through experiment, albeit an experiment that is closely monitored and whose effects are examined and discussed. A client who has gained insight into their reasons for drinking, and who has been involved in the choices and decisions that led to that understanding, is far more likely to sustain any resulting behavioural change in relation to alcohol.

Another reason for working non-directively is that many clients are unable initially to contemplate the prospect of abstinence. Working with goals to reduce consumption gradually might seem more achievable and confidence gained from any evidence of success can make abstinence seem less daunting.

It is important to be clear that a non-directive approach does not imply a lack of structure, although it might well involve more discussion and the need to renegotiate and redefine goals relating to changing patterns of drinking. It does however place the onus upon the client to decide on a course of action and develop the wherewithal to carry it out, skills which can lead towards autonomy and self-management. It also involves learning to monitor how one thinks and feels, particularly in relation to triggers for drinking, as well as developing the flexibility and confidence to change direction quickly when the need arises – a key skill in avoiding relapse.

It is worth explaining to clients that most people who have had an alcohol problem find moderate or controlled drinking more difficult than abstinence, mainly because success and failure with regard to the latter are entirely clear, whereas controlled drinking provides endless scope for the blurring of boundaries and therefore requires ongoing forethought and vigilance to be successful.

Although, as suggested, this way of working can require patience and forbearance on the part of the counsellor, there is also onus on the client to show that the changes they hope to make are achievable. The counsellor may come to feel after a period of time that a particular client will be unable either to drink moderately or to achieve abstinence via a period of controlled drinking. If this is the case it is both appropriate and authentic to admit this honestly to the client, and, if they are willing, to explore other options such as detoxification. A non-directive approach requires congruence but not collusion.

PART II

THE THERAPEUTIC PROCESS: A LINEAR DESCRIPTION

5

FIRST SESSION/ ASSESSMENT

In this chapter we will outline a holistic model for assessing older people who present for counselling to address alcohol problems. We will explain why it is necessary to create trust and safety and will also describe the particular significance of boundaries for this client group. We will describe why assessment should be viewed as a foundational aspect of the therapeutic process and offer a set of tools that will enable the counsellor to gather specific information regarding the client's past and present relationship with alcohol.

ASSESSMENT AND ENGAGEMENT

The process of engagement can often begin before assessment takes place. Where self-referral is an option, clients seeking help might make initial contact by phone, or even occasionally by letter or email. It is also not uncommon for clients to initiate contact via a third party, perhaps a partner, family member or friend. Specialist alcohol agencies normally also take referrals from other statutory or non-statutory services via healthcare professionals and care workers, who will usually have already begun to work with the client in their respective capacities.

Whatever the means of approach, it represents an opportunity to begin to engage the client, even if vicariously, and hence to offer containment and reassurance. It also represents an opportunity to decide whether it is appropriate to offer an assessment at this point and if so to describe in simple terms the assessment process and any initial boundary agreements in relation to such matters as refraining from drinking for an agreed period prior to the first meeting. For clients who are frail or isolated it is also helpful to discuss transport arrangements to the premises, or perhaps to explore whether it is possible for someone to accompany them on their initial visit. Some services offer home visits for clients whose mobility problems or mental health problems prevent them from travelling, and where this is the case it is helpful to explain what conditions need to be in place for the work to be safe and effective. Any preliminary contact represents an opportunity to enable the client seeking help a better opportunity to access the service and to begin to use it effectively.

Assessment has two main purposes. It represents the beginning of a process of gathering information in order to build an understanding of the client's current life situation, personal history, and relationship with alcohol. It also represents the beginning of the therapeutic relationship and hence the opportunity to start to develop trust and clarity with regard to the purpose of the work and the framework in which it will proceed. This is true whether the assessor continues to work with the client when assessment is complete or refers elsewhere. It is especially true if the assessment represents the client's first attempt to find help.

It is important to remember that clients, and particularly those who have had no previous experience of counselling or related activities, may struggle to share information that they consider sensitive or shameful. For this reason the gathering of information, while necessary and important, should not overshadow the need to create a relationship based on trust and safety. Therefore ideally it should be possible to spread the assessment over two sessions. Although in practice this may rarely be needed, it can be very helpful to offer more time to clients who are confused or reticent, or conversely whose need to tell their story temporarily overrides the possibility of asking a full range of specific questions.

Information gained during assessment should not necessarily be regarded as a comprehensive or even totally accurate record of the client's past and present circumstances. Confusion, shyness, memory loss, shame or lack of self-awareness can all prevent clients from sharing the personal and factual information that the assessment process is designed to gather. Much depends upon the skill of the assessor. Sometimes general or oblique questions yield more information than directness. A tactful and sensitive approach can help to lessen any sense of intrusiveness the client might feel when being asked about matters that are unavoidably personal and emotive. Also, while it is important to gain as full a picture as possible, it is equally important to remember that inevitably more information will be gained if the counselling work proceeds, particularly if it can evolve into a mutual and collaborative exploration of the client's life and the place of alcohol within it.

ASSESSMENT AND CONTRACTING

When beginning to work with clients with alcohol problems it is important to have a clear protocol regarding boundaries. Clear agreements regarding issues such as confidentiality, timekeeping and attendance are essential in any counselling work; they can offer valuable reassurance and help to engender trust. However, boundary agreements can have particular therapeutic significance for clients with alcohol problems for a variety of reasons. Confidentiality is especially important in this work because of the shame that so often attaches to alcohol, particularly if the client's drinking contains elements of secrecy. Furthermore boundary agreements, regarding both the counselling relationship and the client's drinking patterns, can be used as a creative tool within therapy. The process of agreeing boundaries, which in this work can often involve definition and redefinition as the work evolves, can help the client to learn to recognise and implement structures in relation to their lifestyle and drinking. This is particularly valuable in the case of clients who present initially as chaotic. Therefore it is very important to involve the client actively from the outset when negotiating boundaries. We will say more about this at a later point.

Clarity regarding confidentiality arrangements is particularly important when clients have been referred by other agencies such as GP surgeries, community mental health units, social services or hospitals. Where this is the case the referrer might also hope to share information regarding the client's progress and welfare as the work proceeds. Frequently work with this client group is more likely to involve collaboration with others. This is particularly so with clients who also have a diagnosed mental health problem or dementia, or a physical illness for which they are currently being treated, and which may be affected by their use of alcohol. In such cases a client in the

UK might be referred as part of their Care Programme Approach: an overall package of care arranged for an individual by a keyworker, which might involve services from both the statutory and voluntary sectors (Department of Health 2008).

It is not possible to describe a set formula for negotiating confidentiality arrangements as these will be influenced by a number of factors, including:

- the policies of the workplace, including those relating to such issues as duty of care, child protection, protection of vulnerable adults, as well as specific confidentiality policies

- the particular needs of the client group and of individual clients who may require flexibility in addition to clarity

- whether the client is being counselled in an agency setting and hence might also be attending groups or other activities within that setting

- whether the work is expected to involve only individual counselling (as might be the case in private practice), or whether it is likely to involve sharing information with other agencies or healthcare professionals.

In the latter case we suggest it is best to be as specific as possible regarding what information is shared, when and with whom, and, where feasible, to gain fresh consent on each occasion of sharing. As an additional safeguard it is normally advisable to ask for written consent (which is usually a requirement in most workplaces involving alcohol and substance misuse counselling).

Although we realise that some counsellors prefer not to undertake a formal assessment, because such an idea conflicts with their theoretical background, we would recommend doing so for the following reasons:

- As mentioned above, the assessment process provides a useful context to involve the client in the process of agreeing appropriate boundaries, including agreements relating to abstinence (some agencies ask clients to abstain from drinking for 12 hours prior to a session, while some – normally those undertaking detox or rehab – insist on total abstinence). It is generally not advisable to try to counsel a client while they are under the influence of alcohol.

- Boundary agreements can include discussing methods and times of contact (i.e. by letter or phone), which safeguard confidentiality, as well as the best time of day to attend (a client who struggles to abstain during the day might prefer a morning session).

- The assessment process also allows the counsellor and client to negotiate the initial frequency of sessions, a factor that can be of particular significance for this client group as it determines a level of support to meet the client's presenting need and also helps to establish therapeutic momentum. This can be especially helpful for clients who are trying not to relapse either by their own efforts or following detoxification.

- It provides an opportunity to gain a broad picture of the client's current situation, family and support network, cultural background and personal history, all of which can have a bearing on their use of alcohol.

- It helps to clarify the client's reasons for coming to counselling, their hopes, expectations and desired outcomes of therapy, and therefore might represent the client's first formal opportunity to explore how they hope to change their drinking.

- It provides an opportunity to collate information which could, with client permission, be used for further referral, if appropriate.

- It provides an opportunity to assess risk to the client (i.e. suicidal ideation, self-harm, psychiatric history, physical health) and to others, including the counsellor him/herself.

With regard to the latter point we strongly suggest negotiating an agreement whereby, if extreme concerns emerge regarding the client's wellbeing or safety, it is possible to contact the client's doctor in general practice (GP), other healthcare professionals or a carer or carers who are involved with the client and/or a third party nominated by the client with such a contingency in mind. This will enable the counsellor, as well as any agency which may employ them, to make every effort to safeguard the client's welfare and to be seen to be doing so. It also allows the counsellor to make enquiries with the aim of trying to ensure continuity at times when the client may be in danger of dropping out. If permission regarding such contingencies is negotiated during initial contracting it prevents the risk of confusion or accusation later, by allowing a clear course of agreed action. This type of agreement is an aspect of the duty of care which the counsellor and any agency they work for has towards the client (please also see Part III, 'Working with Complex Needs/Dual Diagnosis').

As already mentioned, it might sometimes prove necessary to extend the assessment process into a further session, and in practice the amount and accuracy of information shared at this early stage may vary considerably. Nevertheless, it is important to gain as clear a picture as possible regarding the client's current patterns of drinking and about their history of alcohol use, although in many cases this will only become fully apparent as the work proceeds. It is also quite likely that the client's rationale for starting to drink will differ from their reasons for continuing to do so. In addition external factors relating to the client's use of alcohol may have changed during the span in which drinking has been problematic.

Examples presenting at assessment might include:

- the client who has drunk heavily and continuously for more than 20 years, and whose family contains successive generations of people with alcohol problems

- the client whose use of alcohol has changed over an extended period of time, for instance from moderate drinking to heavy problematic drinking to abstinence to bingeing

- the client who used alcohol moderately throughout their adult life then began to drink problematically following a life changing event such as retirement or bereavement

- the client with an alcohol problem of recent onset and relatively short duration who previously had no experience of alcohol use, perhaps because of their cultural or religious background

- the client who has more than one substance dependency but who seeks help specifically with alcohol

- the client whose drinking occurs partially or totally in secret

- the client who feels that their use of alcohol is a metaphor for other needs, for instance someone who has been prone to extremes in several areas of life and who believes that moderate drinking would symbolise the attainment of balance

- the 'dual diagnosis' client who also has a mental illness or a dementia which influences their use of alcohol.

These illustrations may give some indication of the variety of types of drinking, patterns of drinking and reasons for drinking one may encounter. The additional potential for variety in personal, family and professional histories, as well as cultural backgrounds, underlines the importance of obtaining as clear and detailed a picture as possible of the factors which influence a client's relationship with alcohol.

The following are some specific questions which might be asked to elicit a more detailed understanding of the client's use of alcohol.

Long term

Estimated weekly intake (translate into units) This is often an approximation but will give some indication of the severity of the presenting problem, and also whether it is medically safe for a client wishing to do so to try to abstain by their own efforts, or whether a detoxification programme would be necessary, as abrupt abstention can sometimes induce seizure.
Age when started drinking This may reveal something of the client's earliest experiences of alcohol. Was it consumed regularly in the home? Did any other family members have an alcohol problem? Or did the client start to drink late in life and therefore miss the opportunity to learn about safe use?
Age when drinking became a problem In combination with the question above this can help reveal whether the problem developed over a period of time or whether it was triggered by a specific life event or series of events.

Length of problem drinking

This can give some indication of whether moderate drinking is a viable option (for late onset drinkers with a short history of problem drinking this may be the case). For some long term drinkers harm minimisation may be the most realistic goal.

Long term drinking pattern

For example, continuous drinking, intake gradually increasing, sharp increases in intake, binges with abstinent intervals, binges increasing in frequency/length/intensity. Changes in drinking patterns often accompany significant life events.

Longest period of abstinence since problem began

Any evidence of control suggests greater likelihood of a positive outcome.

Do they have any previous experience of counselling/ psychotherapy/alcohol services?

If so it is useful to explore any preconceptions that might have accrued, particularly in relation to boundary agreements in alcohol agencies, as these can vary considerably.

Current

Drinking pattern in the last month

- Voluntary abstinence.
- Involuntary abstinence (for instance because of hospitalisation).
- Heavy drinking sessions throughout week.
- Heavy weekend session drinking.
- Near abstinence/minor drinking episodes.
- Moderate drinking.
- Prolonged bouts/abstinent intervals.
- Continuous drinking through the day.

As well as current usage, this can indicate any recent changes in patterns of drinking.

What drinks are used most frequently?

This can give some indication of how indiscriminate (or otherwise) the client has become in regard to their use of alcohol, although the variety of drinks can also be influenced by financial factors and by simple choice.

Does the client use other harmful or addictive substances?

It is possible that the client is trying to meet separate needs via alcohol and other substances. It is also possible that they are trying to meet the same need/s in a different way. This question might also throw some light on any propensity to generally addictive behaviour.

What are the client's aims in relation to alcohol at the time of assessment?

- To reduce intake.

- To become a social or 'normal' drinker.

- To learn controlled drinking.

- Complete abstinence.

As mentioned above, clients often change or adapt their aims during the course of the work. This in itself can be a valuable aspect of the therapeutic process.

What else does the client hope to achieve at the time of assessment?

- To change social patterns involving alcohol.

- To repair relationships damaged by alcohol use.

- To learn self care and self-management skills.

- To reduce anxiety and/or panic.

- To reduce depression.

- To cope with bereavement.

- To develop confidence or raise self-esteem.

'Subsidiary' goals such as these are likely to be integral to the client's aims regarding their alcohol use.

Generally speaking, any evidence that the problem is contained, that it is boundaried or structured rather than chaotic, suggests greater likelihood of a positive outcome. It is worth pointing out at this stage that if, for instance, a client is only drinking at certain times of day, they are already applying boundaries and thereby demonstrating a measure of control.

A final aspect of assessment relates to protocols regarding maintaining abstinence before and during the counselling session. As already mentioned, we believe that it is not possible to participate effectively in counselling while under the influence of alcohol. We recommend asking clients to refrain from drinking for 12 hours prior to each session. Clients who struggle to do this could be offered morning appointments. If they are unable to comply with this another possibility would be to arrange detox and offer an appointment as soon as possible after this is complete.

6

WORKING WITH TYPES AND PATTERNS OF DRINKING

In this chapter we will define the terms 'alcohol dependency' and 'problematic drinking' as they are used in this book. We will outline the most common types and patterns of drinking and examine their characteristics and aetiology. We will also explore the relationship between types or patterns of drinking and identifying realistic outcomes when helping clients to clarify goals such as abstinence, moderate drinking or harm minimisation.

The term *alcohol dependency* has acquired a variety of meanings. It is used throughout this book to describe an inability to refrain from drinking, either generally or within given circumstances. It also describes a relationship with alcohol in which drinking represents an attempt to meet significant personal needs, whether consciously or unconsciously. It is used as a general term and not as a distinction to indicate a more serious or complex level or form of drinking from other less harmful manifestations.

In the context of this book the term *problematic drinking* is used to describe drinking that is in any way harmful or which causes an appreciable level of difficulty to the drinker or to those around them.

Alcohol dependency may either precede or coincide with problematic drinking. This will depend upon factors such as the contexts in which drinking occurs and whether consumption increases gradually or abruptly.

TYPES AND PATTERNS OF DRINKING

There are many ways to categorise types of problematic drinking. What follows is a description of the more recognisable forms that it can take, and the characteristics that are most likely to accompany them.

Broadly speaking older people who present with alcohol problems can be divided into two categories:

1. *Long term*: Problematic drinking began (relatively) early in life and has continued with or without periods of abstinence. Where this is the case, patterns of drinking may have varied over the course of time, and it may be possible to link changes in patterns to life events. Older drinkers, because of their age, are more likely to present with a longer history of problematic drinking.

2. *Late onset*: Problematic drinking began later in life, often triggered by specific events such as illness, retirement or bereavement. This usually manifests as a gradual or abrupt increase in consumption in a previously moderate drinker. Occasionally it occurs when a previous non-drinker is introduced to alcohol at a time of trauma or difficulty.

LONG TERM DRINKING

Defining what represents 'long term' drinking can be somewhat arbitrary. We feel that two factors are most relevant:

- the actual time span of dependent or problematic drinking

- the proportion that this represents within the context of an individual's overall life span.

The second factor is particularly relevant for older people. A 25-year-old with a seven-year history of problematic drinking will have been coping with the problem for all of their adult life. For a 65-year-old a similar span will represent a far smaller proportion. This is significant for a variety of reasons:

- such a person can call upon many years of life experience during which their use of alcohol caused no difficulty or ill effect

- these years may contain the experience of moderate drinking or abstinence, and hence evidence of previous ability to control consumption

- problematic drinking that begins in maturity is less likely to result from or be reinforced by peer pressure (this point also relates to late onset drinking).

We would therefore suggest that, for people aged 55 or over, problematic drinking could be defined as long term when it has lasted for ten years or more. There can be little doubt that after this length of time it will represent an entrenched behaviour with potentially significant consequences. Our experience suggests that a long term drinker, by this definition, can rarely if ever revert to moderate drinking, although they may learn much by trying to do so. Nevertheless clients who fall into this category may still benefit from an approach aiming at harm minimisation, that is help to reduce to a level at which damage to health and other consequences are not as severe, if abstinence has proved impossible to achieve.

Older people whose problematic drinking began early in life face a greater range and degree of challenges. Here the span of drinking, whether or not it has been always been viewed as a problem by the client, may be anything between 20 and 50 years, and it is likely that all aspects of the client's life will be affected by their drinking. In extreme cases day-to-day life may be arranged entirely around the need to drink. In such instances any attempt to stop will involve major adjustments or perhaps even a complete change of lifestyle.

LATE ONSET DRINKING

The term 'late onset' is usually used to describe drinking that has become problematic in late middle age or early old age. Typically the duration of the problem will be relatively brief, for example two years or less, and hence the onset more recent at the point where the client presents for counselling. In such instances, if the problem has not become too intense, it may be realistic for the client to return to moderate drinking, ideally after a period of abstinence, should they so choose. This is especially possible if they have used alcohol moderately throughout their adult life. However, anyone who has developed an alcohol dependency and who subsequently attempts to drink moderately will always need to remain vigilant and be aware of the possibility of relapse or escalation into problematic drinking.

Because problematic drinking that begins later in life presents a recognisable and usually unmistakeable contrast to what has gone before, this type of drinker is more likely to seek help, or be advised to seek help, earlier than long term drinkers, especially as the latter often develop sophisticated coping strategies that serve to mask their problem. Sometimes, however, difficulties arising from late onset drinking are not acknowledged until the problem has become more entrenched. This is particularly likely for solitary drinkers. An example might be someone who lives alone, takes early retirement and, deprived of the structure of a working day, begins to drink more to alleviate boredom. Retirement can offer such a person relative anonymity in contrast to the world of work, where a drink problem is more likely to become apparent to others and to be remarked upon.

Another frequent causal factor in late onset drinking is bereavement. Here also the problem may not be immediately apparent to others, as people who drink more because they have lost a loved one often do so in solitude. Ironically in this type of situation alcohol is likely to inhibit the full expression of grief, and thus also the natural momentum of the grieving process.

Where late onset drinking is a response to specific life events the client will benefit most if both their drinking and the event or events which led to it are addressed. In the above examples a client struggling to adapt to retirement might be encouraged to explore activities that give shape and meaning to their daily existence. A bereaved client might benefit from bereavement counselling, either as a component of the alcohol work or as a complementary activity, taking place alongside it.

Both long term and late onset drinking may take a variety of forms. The following are some types and patterns of drinking that present most frequently.

Continual heavy drinking

This term refers to heavy drinking that takes place each day, with few if any abstinent days between. It applies to drinking that takes place in only part of each day as well as drinking that takes place throughout the entire day.

This pattern is least likely to be accompanied by self-awareness. People who drink heavily on a daily basis are rarely able to process their feelings, to reflect on their reasons for drinking or to deal effectively with life events. Drinkers who fall into this category are most likely to need detoxification and to experience significant and perhaps dangerous withdrawal symptoms if they try to stop abruptly or without medical help.

People who drink continually can be very difficult to engage in counselling, not least because they often struggle to refrain from drinking prior to counselling sessions. It is not possible to offer effective counselling to people who are intoxicated. A practical solution here can be to offer such clients an early morning appointment, as long as they are not also drinking during the night. If this is not possible (heavy drinkers are often unable to rise early), another possible option is to arrange detoxification, providing the client is willing, before counselling takes place (see Chapter 8, 'Detoxification (Detox)').

Clients who drink heavily but whose drinking conforms to a pattern can be somewhat easier to engage, particularly if drinking is regularly contained within a certain part of the day. It is worth pointing out to such clients that their use of alcohol, however damaging, already contains evidence of self-control because by its nature takes place within a regular time boundary. For this reason it is also more likely to be amenable to incremental reduction.

Binge drinking

The term 'bingeing' is usually applied to heavy and uncontrolled bouts of occasional drinking which are interspersed with abstinent periods or, more rarely, periods or instances of moderate drinking.

There are two types of binge drinking:

1. *Chaotic bingeing*: Drinking is heavy but sporadic. Binges may occur in the context of an otherwise ordered life, or as a further expression of chaos within a generally chaotic life pattern. This is probably the most difficult form of drinking to work with because of its unpredictability, because it can be

hard to identify triggers or because triggers are often many and varied.

2. *Bingeing that conforms to a pattern or that occurs in response to specific events*: This type of drinking can vary considerably in frequency but tends to be easier to work with because it is usually possible to anticipate the likelihood of instances of bingeing.

For some drinkers any alcohol intake will escalate immediately into a binge. For others the progression will be inevitable but more gradual. Occasionally it is possible to meet binge drinkers who are able to drink moderately on occasions, or even most of the time, without this leading to bingeing. Where this is the case binges usually occur in response to very specific triggers and often represent an attempt to escape fear or emotional pain stemming from either current or past events or situations.

Triggers for bingeing can vary considerably and can be both external and internal, that is they can relate to an event or to a thought or feeling. It could also be argued that this distinction is arbitrary, as in practice the two are usually interlinked, with events provoking the thoughts and feelings that lead to bingeing and vice versa. When trying to establish the specific circumstances that act as triggers, however, it can be helpful to explore the exact sequence that led to the binge and hence whether any related event precedes or follows the thoughts and feelings it is linked with. In the first instance it may be possible for the client to avoid the particular circumstance that they find disturbing or to learn to approach it differently. In the latter case the thoughts and feelings themselves can be recognised as causal and addressed accordingly.

Anniversaries of bereavements or of birthdays or dates that are particularly associated with lost loved ones are typical events that may trigger bingeing in older people. Here binges are likely to be spaced far apart and may even only occur annually. Christmas, so heavily associated with alcohol in western cultures, is another emotive time and one in which drinkers of all descriptions are vulnerable to relapse. Older people may also binge before, after or during situations that cause them anxiety or to feel unsafe.

As already mentioned, when working with people who binge it is helpful to make every effort to establish the specific triggers for drinking where this is possible. It is also important to explore whether there has been any accumulation of thoughts, feelings or events that have contributed to the need to binge. Binge drinking often represents an attempt to relieve psychological pressure or to remove oneself psychologically from situations that cause distress. This type of drinker will benefit from anything that helps them to cope with feelings of pressure, including ways to prevent these accumulating. Encouraging the practice of daily relaxation can be extremely valuable, as can anything that enables the client to speak about and process feelings.

It is also sometimes possible to identify earlier instances in the personal history of binge drinkers in which the habit of repressing feelings was learned or developed. Perhaps this felt like the only way of coping at the time and thus represented an appropriate response to an otherwise overwhelming situation. Where this has been the case clients may find healing in the trust, safety and hence opportunity to speak openly that the counselling relationship provides. It is also worth exploring different ways in which to view and respond to pressure situations. Clients may find that they have developed, or are able to develop, greater resources with which to deal with such situations.

Binge drinkers are especially prone to mood swings. Because of this they can benefit from learning to be aware of and to anticipate abrupt changes in mood, where these are seen to trigger binges. All-consuming despondency and unrealistic optimism are both typical characteristics and can prevent such clients from responding to their circumstances in a measured way. No category of drinker is more likely to globalise their current mood and so be unable to see beyond it. Clients displaying this type of volatility should be encouraged to speak to their GP, in case medication might offer an appropriate form of help. Needless to say alcohol is likely to exacerbate such volatility, and abstinence can help to reduce mood swings, as can regular habits in relation to self-care (see Chapter 7, 'Addressing the Problem: Alcohol and the Hierarchy of Needs').

A final characteristic that is common to most binge drinkers is impulsiveness. Some may exhibit impetuosity in their general behaviour, others only in regard to their relationship with alcohol. Binge drinkers who have relapsed frequently describe either an overwhelming impulse to drink which they felt unable to resist or a moment of irrationality in which they imagined that it would be safe to take a single drink or a certain type of drink. Recent research validates this difficulty by suggesting that, where there is an established addiction, exposure to an addictive substance can reduce activity in the part of the brain that can override impulsivity. When this occurs the rational mind is effectively bypassed or overwhelmed, resulting in far greater likelihood of relapse (Lemonick and Park 2007). Certainly the testimony of many binge drinkers bears this out, and we believe that it is a mistake to regard descriptions of this type of behaviour as a simple excuse.

The common feature of this type of scenario is the speed with which the impulse arises and is yielded to. This is another reason why it is so difficult to work with. Again it can be helpful to explore the characteristics of the impulse and the situations in which it takes place. Progress can be made if the drinker can create space between the impulse, which is often fleeting if not yielded to, and the desire to respond to it.

Other encouraging signs are:

- where the client is able to identify triggers clearly or to develop insight into other reasons for drinking

- where the client begins to be able to eliminate or resist certain triggers

- where there are longer spaces between binges

- where binges become shorter or less severe.

Secret drinking

Secret drinking occurs when the drinker, on a regular basis, makes a conscious attempt to hide their drinking from others. This should be distinguished from the more common practice of under reporting how much is consumed.

Secret drinking is frequently accompanied by shame, fear at prospect of discovery and reluctance to admit the need behind the drinking. It can occur alongside apparently normal social drinking, in which case each type of drinking might arise from a different motive. It can sometimes occur in response to the disapproval of others.

This form of drinking can be particularly complex to work with, partly because the motivation for the actual drinking frequently differs from the motivation for concealing it. Also, by its nature, it is systemic: the drinker wishes to hide what they are doing from others. Therefore the attitudes of those from whom the drinker wishes to conceal their drinking can be a significant factor in working with the problem. Typically disapproval only compounds the need to hide. This may be because it is experienced as additional pressure, because the drinking becomes a form of rebellion or because the drinker experiences a sense of thrill in concealing an activity that others would forbid and the thrill itself becomes an incentive. Of course the drinker might have legitimate reason to fear the disapproval of others, for instance the prospect of violence or abuse.

Some drinkers of this type consider the act of secrecy, rather than the actual drinking, to be their main problem, and indeed sometimes the amount consumed can be relatively small. Here the need to conceal certain behaviours may be rooted in past experience, or the secrecy might represent an aspect of the dynamics of a current relationship with a partner or with family.

Work with this type of problem can be protracted and can require much patience. As stated, secret drinkers typically incur disapproval and it is very important for the counsellor to maintain an attitude of acceptance, however much this is tested. It is also important to remember that simply enabling this type of client to admit their drinking represents a considerable breakthrough. Also, that as soon as the clandestine activity is spoken about, the element of secrecy and the pressure this creates for the client begins to be diluted.

It can be helpful to explore gently what lies behind the need to hide. When did it begin? How did it develop? Alongside this it is valuable to gain a clear sense of the client's relationship with alcohol and with the person or people from whom they hide their drinking. Is the habit of secrecy generalised or specific to the use of alcohol? Shame is endemic in this type of drinking and an unconditional attitude on the part of the counsellor, which does not preclude the maintenance of clear boundaries, can have a disproportionate effect in facilitating a positive outcome.

The work may also involve negotiation, both between the counsellor and client, and between the client and those from whom they hide their drinking, who in practice are likely to be at least partially aware of what is happening. This might for instance involve discussing ways to facilitate the gradual transition to controlled drinking in the company of others, for example at evening meals. It might also involve enabling the client, where this is possible, to speak about what has driven them to secrecy in relation to those who are affected by their drinking. Sometimes this can reveal issues relating to control, or the feeling of being controlled. There may also be collusion, for instance where the secret drinking is known about but ignored, or come to be regarded as 'normal'.

Finally it is sometimes the case that secret drinking represents a component of a more generalised problem with alcohol. One possible approach here is to address the respective aspects of the client's drinking in stages, for instance agreeing an initial aim of eliminating secret drinking before addressing whatever other forms the drinking might take.

Ritualised drinking

This type of drinking occurs when the use of alcohol is combined over a long period with relatively fixed and repetitive forms of behaviour. Therefore both alcohol and the behaviours it accompanies become part of a clearly defined and mutually sustaining habit.

Much of our identity derives from the simple habits of our lives. Perhaps this becomes even more true as we grow older. Many retired people, for instance, develop habitual patterns of activities as a way of structuring their time. It is also not uncommon for older people to develop 'rituals', by which we mean regularly repeated habits or structured behaviour, that come to have personal significance. They may do the same thing at the same time every day or on certain days, perhaps deriving an ancillary sense of pleasure, comfort or safety in enacting a clearly defined routine. Where alcohol is involved these repetitive patterns can serve to reinforce the habit of drinking and create, as if by stealth, dependency. Often alcohol and the enactment and re-enactment of the routine become equally important, and one would be deprived of significance in the absence of the other. This type of scenario may even evolve to the point where the ritual eventually revolves entirely around the need to drink.

It is important to realise that, like most activities, if this pattern is repeated frequently and for sufficient duration it will eventually be experienced as normal. Hence its absence would create a double sense of deprivation: that of the drinking and that of the activity that accompanies it.

Surprisingly, as it usually presents as an entrenched habit, this type of drink problem can prove relatively easy to work with. Far from being chaotic it is usually predictable in terms of when and where it occurs, what activities accompany it and even with regard to the type and quantity of alcohol that is consumed. Therefore, although initially rituals can seem intractable, the very fact that they are structured and repetitive can make them more amenable to adaptation, change and perhaps eventually discard.

Older people may place great investment in routine and either stopping or reducing intake is likely to involve mental, emotional and behavioural adaptation. The sense of deprivation that clients experience when habits that accompany the activity of drinking are disrupted can be as intense as the loss of alcohol itself.

Usually it is best to try to adapt the ritual slowly, if possible substituting new behaviours that are pleasant and beneficial, and particularly those that will impact on craving or reduce the sense of deprivation. For instance where drinking has accompanied meals, the client might place greater emphasis on their enjoyment of food. They might also substitute a non-alcoholic drink that they particularly like and, where there has been an aesthetic element in the ritual, serve this from a jug or decanter.

Like secret drinking, working with ritualised drinking can involve protracted negotiation between the counsellor and client and, where this is the case, between the client and their partner, family or whoever else might be involved. It is very important to discuss with the client what they feel they can manage at each stage. A process of gradual adaptation, where possible, is more likely to be sustained. In cases where the client simply wishes to reduce, and where their history of drinking and other factors make this feasible, it may be possible for them to keep all other aspects of the ritual intact, or to make minimal changes such as decanting the amount of wine that will accompany a meal before the meal takes place.

If gradual change does not prove possible, the client may find it necessary to stop the activity that accompanies drinking completely, as it would become meaningless in the absence of alcohol or is too strongly associated with the need to drink. This is sometimes the case for clients who have always smoked while drinking or who through long habit have drunk at specific social occasions.

Sometimes also clients wish to make a fresh start and find it easiest to relinquish the ritual abruptly. This may particularly be the case after detox. In such instances it is useful to discuss other possibilities that are meaningful to the client and which might serve as a substitute, again to lessen any sense of loss or deprivation that might lead to relapse.

Associative drinking

This term describes a type of drinking that is triggered when alcohol is associated involuntarily with a particular situation, event or circumstance, by sensory stimuli such as taste, smell or imagery, or by specific thoughts or patterns of thoughts.

Alcohol has become so heavily associated with a wide variety of social contexts that the provision and sharing of alcohol could reasonably be described as an endemic aspect of western culture. A plethora of entrenched links have developed, sometimes over many centuries, between alcohol and specific social situations, particularly those involving leisure and celebration. As an obvious example, in most western cultures a wedding reception without alcohol would almost certainly be greeted with surprise and, doubtless more often than not, disappointment.

When working with people who develop alcohol problems it soon becomes apparent that these associations, while undoubtedly deriving from a broader context, can often become highly personalised and even idiosyncratic. They may also be unpredictable and sporadic and therefore difficult to anticipate. Furthermore, associations which act as triggers for drinking frequently become so assimilated that the person who is subject to experiencing them is unaware of their potential influence until they are triggered. Unsurprisingly, associations that were previously effectively unconscious often come to light during the initial phases of abstinence, when clients typically become acutely aware of stimuli that relate to the desire to drink alcohol. This type of association can be accompanied by a sense of longing and loss, by powerful craving, or both. Such feelings, although normally transient, can prove overwhelming at the point at which they are experienced. Binge drinkers can be particularly vulnerable to relapse in such instances.

There are also of course more generalised associations to which clients remain vulnerable. As already mentioned, those in the early stages of abstinence frequently become particularly conscious of the preponderance of alcohol in general society and the media. Advertising invariably stimulates and exploits the concept of association by linking brands of drink to pleasant situations, desirable personality traits or enjoyable states of mind, thereby increasing individual and collective susceptibility. Furthermore many well known creative and charismatic people are and have been heavy drinkers, often creating an unfortunate precedent for those who would wish to emulate them but who are unable to distinguish between talent and glamour and the behaviours that sometimes accompany it.

Other very common associations are those between smoking and alcohol, and between alcohol and mealtimes. These could be described as repetitive associations and can represent an aspect of ritualistic drinking, whereby their very predictability makes them somewhat easier to anticipate and thus prepare for. Less frequent, but extremely powerful in their potential to trigger relapse, are the associations between days of national celebration, such as Christmas, New Year's Eve and, for many, St Patrick's Day. Here the association with alcohol can be amplified by a feeling of being excluded from celebration that accompanies festivities, by virtue of not wishing to drink. It is well worth entering into specific and detailed preparation with clients who might be vulnerable at such times. It is also worth asking the question: 'How might you be able to celebrate without alcohol?' Clients who are unable to envisage such a possibility may find it best simply to avoid situations in which the temptation to drink is likely to prove irresistible. Paradoxically clients who are attempting to drink moderately may cope better with these situations, as the fact that they are able to drink even a small amount may lessen any sense of exclusion.

It is also common for clients to experience strong cravings for alcohol when eating certain types of food. In such cases the association can be very specific indeed and, if it relates to foods that are not encountered regularly, can come as a surprise, particularly if cravings that accompany the association prove very strong.

A general rule when working with associations that have the potential to trigger relapse is to help the client anticipate the likelihood of their occurrence where possible. Experience counts for a great deal here, especially when working with clients who have only recently become abstinent and who are still in the early stages of learning about their individual relationship with alcohol. By paying close attention to clients' descriptions of relevant factors in their personal history and lifestyle the counsellor is often more able to be aware of potential difficulties than the client, and a practical exploration of possible coping strategies before a foreseeable contingency can prove extremely valuable in helping to avoid relapse. As abstinence is consolidated, spontaneous impulses to drink are likely to decrease in frequency and may also decrease in strength. Similarly the client's ability to recognise and resist such impulses is likely to increase.

Drinking for self-medication

The term self-medication refers to the practice of attempting to derive therapeutic benefit through the use of alcohol. It also refers to instances where alcohol is used as an alternative to prescribed medication.

The idea that alcohol can be used for 'medicinal purposes' has been prevalent within our society for many centuries and continues to the present day. 'Medicinal purposes' in this context could be defined as any circumstance in which people seek to effect beneficial change of a physical, mental or emotional nature through the use of alcohol. Furthermore help of this kind might be sought consciously or unconsciously. In other words the user might be clear as to why they are taking alcohol and what they hope it will achieve, or conversely might be unaware that via drinking they are hoping to gain some kind of therapeutic effect. The issue of self-medication is particularly significant for older clients as they are more likely to have medical conditions that require accurately prescribed medication. The danger of using alcohol as a substitute for proper medical attention is self-evident.

People may use alcohol for the following reasons:

- as an analgesic (to relieve pain or discomfort)

- as a relaxant or sedative (to ease anxiety or to improve sleep)

- as a stimulant (to gain energy, confidence or courage in social situations)

- as an anti-depressant (to act as a 'pick me up', i.e. to raise low mood)

- as a tranquilliser (to alleviate shock or panic).

However, people who are motivated to use alcohol to achieve any of the above normally report that any positive effect is short-lived and that alcohol eventually contributes to their problem, rather than alleviating it. One way this can occur is that alcohol can mask symptoms in their original form so that it becomes necessary to untangle the initial reason/s for drinking from the additional adverse effects of alcohol use. Also, if alcohol is combined with prescribed medication, it can undermine its effectiveness and may result in harmful side effects. For instance, when taken with a painkiller alcohol will reduce the period for which pain is relieved.

The circumstances in which people turn to alcohol can be indicators of an underlying need or needs. Helping to identify these can offer the client the possibility of finding alternative ways of meeting them which do not involve alcohol. It can also of course highlight the need for medical referral. Typical examples include a client who drank to quell the pain of osteoarthritis, a client who drank to cope with the effects of anxiety and a client who drank to alleviate depression.

7

ADDRESSING THE PROBLEM

Alcohol and the Hierarchy of Needs

In this chapter we describe how the principles of Maslow's Hierarchy of Needs can be used as a holistic model to clarify and address clients' issues and needs, with the further intention of helping them to meet these through means that do not involve alcohol. We explore the following areas: physiological needs, safety needs, needs for love, affection and belongingness, needs for esteem and needs for self-actualisation.

One model that can help the therapist to clarify the client's reasons for drinking, as well as the effects of drinking and related issues, is Maslow's Hierarchy of Needs (Maslow 1943). As the term suggests this theory postulates a sequence of needs which are inherent in the human condition, ranging from 'deficiency' or lower needs to 'growth' or higher needs. They are hierarchical in the sense that Maslow believed that each need, starting from the lowest, must be met sufficiently before the one above it can also be genuinely fulfilled (Maslow 1954). Although we do not subscribe rigidly to this aspect of the model, the ability to differentiate between and address levels of need in a co-ordinated way has considerable validity in work involving alcohol, particularly as clients often require practical and emotional support before they are able to engage effectively in therapy. It can be particularly helpful following relapse, when work can involve enabling clients to re-establish basic self-management skills, which can in turn allow them to participate constructively in the process of therapy.

Although Maslow later extended this concept to make further distinctions regarding growth needs, it will suffice here to look at the five needs he outlined initially (Maslow 1943). From lower to higher these are:

- physiological needs

- safety needs

- needs for love, affection and belongingness

- needs for esteem

- self-actualisation needs.

People who develop an alcohol dependency will almost certainly be trying to meet or compensate for the lack of one or more of these needs through the use of alcohol. Using the hierarchy as a template can help the therapist to gain a more specific sense of the need or needs behind the dependency, as well as an indication of what interventions might prove effective in helping the client to meet them. Alcohol dependency stems from unmet needs. When such needs are met dependency invariably reduces.

The following headings cover illustrations from each category in the hierarchy.

PHYSIOLOGICAL NEEDS

Clients with alcohol problems are more prone to physical illness and more likely to neglect their physical wellbeing than the general population (Blondell 2000). The very nature of excessive alcohol consumption suggests a lack of awareness regarding the needs of the body, or possibly an attempt to meet those needs inappropriately. We have referred to one aspect of this, where alcohol is used as a form of self-medication, in the previous chapter.

Experiencing poor health can weaken the resolve of people in the early stages of recovery, when even a mild illness such as a cold can trigger relapse, because of its lowering effect on mood. As well as the intrinsic value of feeling well, the process of acquiring skills that maintain good health involves the development of self-awareness, through learning to sense the body's needs and how to respond to them. In addition, by regularly monitoring their physical and emotional wellbeing, clients dispel the tendency to disassociate from body and feelings so prevalent in those who misuse alcohol. This in turn will help them to become more sensitised to its ill effects. Through attending to the basics of diet, hydration, exercise and sleep the client can form a strong basis from which to proceed.

Diet

Alcohol impairs the breakdown and absorption of nutrients, so people with alcohol problems get less nutritional value from their food (Foster and Marriott 2006). In addition they are more likely to neglect their diet in the first place. Some people drink instead of eating or find that their eating patterns are disrupted because of the way they drink.

Food also has an important part to play in the prevention of relapse. Eating at regular intervals helps to maintain blood sugar levels, which in turn can help to prevent fluctuations in mood that, as already suggested, can trigger relapse. This is particularly so at the beginning of the work when clients are more likely to repeat past behaviours which may often have been driven by a desire for instant relief or gratification. Later, particularly if they have grown more able to accommodate painful or uncomfortable feelings, this need will be less pressing, but the value of good eating remains for maintaining physical wellbeing, because it can help to reduce craving and because it evidences self-management and self care.

Hydration

Alcohol is a diuretic; it takes fluid from the body (as does caffeine, drinks containing which are often used cyclically with alcohol). This has two implications:

1. The diuretic effect is compounded in older people in whom there is a fall in the ratio of body fluid to fat, meaning that there is less water initially for the alcohol to be diluted in, hence its intoxicating effects are likely to be greater.

2. Dehydration, like hunger, induces a sense of deficit. It is necessary to drink water regularly to maintain energy and concentration levels. Good hydration, like good diet, can help to reduce craving, and therefore the danger of relapse in clients who are trying to abstain. It is very important to encourage clients who are still drinking to quench their thirst, ideally with water, before they drink alcohol.

Exercise

Exercise offers both physiological and psychological benefits, some of which can be of particular value to older people who are overcoming alcohol problems. However, it is important to encourage clients who are considering adopting an exercise regime to seek medical advice first, particularly if they have an extensive history of problematic drinking or have recently undergone detoxification. The importance of exercise is now widely recognised within primary care and it is not uncommon for general practitioners to prescribe exercise sessions in addition to or instead of medication. Doctors will also be able to advise regarding contra-indications for exercise. Clients should be aware that alcohol can reduce strength and endurance, and inhibit aerobic capacity during exercise and also the ability to recover afterwards. For this reason it is important that clients who are still drinking are discouraged from taking strenuous exercise after heavy or binge drinking, when their system is still in recovery.

Exercise can be of particular benefit to this client group because:

- regular exercise encourages the development of discipline

- it can help to give structure to the day

- gentle aerobic exercise such as walking and swimming can encourage good breathing, which in turn can help to reduce anxiety and depression

- aerobic exercise also has a cleansing effect on the body

- it involves movement and so can help to counteract the sense of inertia that so often accompanies alcohol problems

- it can help improve sleep (see below).

Sleep

Sleep quality can be impaired by alcohol use in a variety of ways:

- It might take longer to fall asleep (it is common for people to drink to try to initiate sleep).

- Sleep patterns can be disrupted, for instance with frequent awakenings.

- Sleep quality can be adversely affected, so that sleep is less restful and less refreshing.

- In older people alcohol-related sleep deficiencies can be exacerbated by conditions associated with age, for instance the need to empty the bladder and increased sensitivity to noise.

In addition sleep is almost always impaired by an abrupt reduction in alcohol consumption, for instance following detoxification (Landolt and Gillin 2001). This is an important point because the resolve to abstain can be undermined by lack of good quality sleep: it can be a trigger for relapse.

Although the alcohol counsellor cannot be expected to have expert knowledge it can be valuable to explore simple steps to help the client to improve their sleep. Clients whose lifestyle tends to be chaotic can particularly benefit from adopting a consistent sleep regime.

Steps to improve sleep may include:

- reducing the potential for noise in the environment

- sleeping in a darkened room

- ensuring that the bedroom is well ventilated

- refraining from taking fluids for two hours before going to bed

- refraining from eating a heavy meal before going to bed

- going to bed at the same time each night

- trying not to sleep during the day.

Clients who report prolonged difficulty should be advised to consult their doctor.

SAFETY NEEDS

In Chapter 5, 'First Session/Assessment', we gave reasons why boundary agreements can be of particular importance for this client group. Paramount amongst these is the need to create a sense of safety. This entails the development of trust and will be supported by clear agreements in relation to confidentiality. It can take great courage to tell a stranger that you have a problem with alcohol – it is vital that the client feels that such information will be treated with respect and discretion.

The role of the counsellor will inevitably involve witnessing privileged information, including information that may never have been disclosed elsewhere. For some clients a habit of secrecy may attach to the way they drink, their reasons for drinking and to the repercussions of drinking. Fear of sharing matters which shame has kept private can be overcome if the client senses that the counsellor is trustworthy, not judgemental and someone to whom it is possible to speak openly.

In addition to fear of inappropriate disclosure there may be other concerns relating to the interactive aspect of counselling. Clients may worry that they will experience pressure to talk about intimate matters, or that they might inadvertently say something they will later regret. They might be afraid that they will be unable to find words to express their thoughts, feelings or situation, or that what they say will portray them in a bad light, or that aspects of their story might shock. Sometimes clients are anxious not to speak about certain events or areas of their lives. Occasionally a client will 'only want to talk about the alcohol', and will try to treat it as discrete from the rest of their existence. It is also common for clients to fear that what they say will not be believed, perhaps because their experience is unusual, or because they have previously encountered disbelief or scepticism when describing their circumstances.

Much can be done to allay such concerns. It cannot be overstated that clear boundary agreements are particularly important for this client group and it is best to be specific when explaining with whom and for what reason any aspect of the sessions might be shared. Similarly clear agreements about matters such as attendance and timekeeping, because they offer structure, can also offer a sense of containment and hence contribute to the client's ability to feel safe. Nevertheless it is very common for people with alcohol problems to challenge or try to evade such agreements. Alcohol is a great dissolver of boundaries and those who develop alcohol problems have often struggled with boundaries and structure generally throughout their lives. A world lacking structure and clarity can feel very unsafe. Working with these issues is an integral aspect of the therapeutic process and requires much sensitivity and discretion.

Although it is important to gain a broad picture of clients' current circumstances as quickly as possible, particularly anything that influences their use of alcohol, it is also advisable to respect any initial reticence and to allow them to disclose sensitive material at their own pace. Clients sometimes find it easier to examine deeper underlying issues when they have begun to establish some control over their drinking. This can be particularly true of older people, whose drinking may have prevented them from processing issues which go back several decades.

It may also become apparent that external factors compromise a client's ability to feel safe. Heavy drinking can bring about financial problems. There may also be difficulties relating to accommodation, as alcohol abuse can lead to difficulty in paying rent, divorce or separation and hence the need to move away from home, or even to homelessness or periods in a hostel. In other instances a client may currently be in an abusive relationship, or have experienced abuse in the past. It is also common for clients coming out of detoxification to experience panic or anxiety or severe disorientation. Long periods of problematic drinking can also erode personal support systems, and it is not uncommon to meet clients who are socially isolated. This is particularly likely in the case of older people.

For all these reasons it can be extremely valuable to compile a referral list of services that can offer other complementary practical and emotional support. In addition, being able to make effective referrals for clients with complex or multiple needs can significantly ease the burden on the counsellor, particularly if working in private practice. It might also be the case that counsellors working in agencies hold the additional responsibility of keyworking clients and therefore the work will naturally involve formulating a care plan and co-ordinating the client's care.

Another practical step that can help to create safety involves offering clients the opportunity to nominate a 'significant other' in event of concerns for their safety. Clients may of course choose not to pursue this option, and it is advisable to explain that such a course of action would only be pursued in extreme circumstances. However, this type of arrangement can offer reassurance to someone whose drinking is out of control, or someone whose recent personal or medical history points to such a need.

A final point in relation to working with the safety needs of this client group is that much tension that can exist between issues of autonomy and independence and the ongoing need for support, the latter a prevalent feature of work with vulnerable older people. The counsellor, who might hold concerns for a client's welfare or feel frustrated at unwillingness to seek or accept help or take a certain course of action, may at times share the tension inherent in this apparent dichotomy. The challenge when this occurs is to simply stay alongside the client in their decision making process. It is crucial to witness the client's experience and perspective and to provide space for them to reflect and explore options, though this might be a slow process involving much repetition. A patient and facilitative approach will often enable the client to resolve such issues in their own way and to their own satisfaction. In addition, the constancy this stance demonstrates will provide its own form of safety and can create a climate in which it is easier to work with any dependency the client may have developed upon the counselling relationship itself when the work nears its end.

NEEDS FOR LOVE, AFFECTION AND BELONGINGNESS

As already suggested, one of the foremost social dangers of prolonged alcohol use is its tendency to result in isolation, or at least to deplete natural resources of support which family, friends and contacts within the community might provide. It can also erode the respect and affection of those closest to the drinker, who may become frustrated or hostile in reaction to the behavioural changes that can accompany problematic drinking.

Paradoxically, the desire to be close to others, and the attempt to achieve this through alcohol, often proves to be the first step towards problem drinking. Although this is normally far from being a considered or indeed rational process at the time it takes place, in retrospect clients have suggested that they used alcohol for the following reasons:

- to reduce shyness or inhibition

- to overcome boredom and loneliness

- to dissolve barriers that prevent intimacy

- to enhance companionship

- to facilitate a sense of belongingness

- to aid seduction.

A difficulty that accompanies this sort of motivation is that people who pursue such possibilities through drinking can come to believe that it is essential to use alcohol to realise and sustain them. Therefore the absence of alcohol becomes associated with loneliness and inadequacy. From here the path to dependency is clear cut. Ironically it is also common for this type of drinker to conclude eventually that intimacy or companionship that is achieved through the use of alcohol is of poor quality and ultimately unsatisfying.

What does this signify in terms of the counselling process? First, the counsellor will be meeting the client at times when they are sober. Thus their relationship, which by its nature has considerable elements of intimacy, will be conducted without the immediate influence of alcohol, and so has the potential to model a way of relating that does not depend on alcohol to be meaningful, satisfying and authentic.

It is also important to gain an understanding of what represents intimacy to the individual client. Place within the family, the sharing of daily rituals, sexuality and sensuality, physical proximity, kindred interests, intellectual compatibility and shared spiritual beliefs are among the ways in which we find and maintain closeness, also through which we express love and affection and experience a sense of belonging. The degree of meaning and importance that individuals attach to each of these aspects can vary considerably. In exploring such matters in a counselling setting it is advisable to be tentative, as it is not uncommon for people with a long history of alcohol dependency to feel that they have never experienced genuine intimacy, or have lost the ability to do so. In an older client group it is especially likely that the subject of intimacy will be associated with loss.

It is sometimes possible to develop a sense of what the client experiences as intimacy, and of how they express intimacy, through their interaction within the counselling setting. It may also be possible to gain insight into how an individual may avoid or forfeit intimacy, or indeed drink to escape it.

Working with lost or impoverished intimacy often involves a re-evaluation of relationships or of attitudes toward relationships. Sometimes the client may decide that it is necessary to discard previous harmful relationships and to seek a new social network that is not held together by alcohol. This can be a considerable challenge for an older person, who might not have the range of contacts, or means of making contacts, that are available to someone younger. This scenario is particularly likely in people who have experienced homelessness because of their drinking, who may find that they need to rebuild all aspects of their lives.

Alternatively it is sometimes the case that relationships can be reframed, or put on a more viable or satisfying basis. Sometimes this can happen naturally. For instance a client whose son changed from calling him 'Dad' to 'Dave' during the most difficult part of his alcohol use reverted to 'Dad' when things improved. Another not uncommon example is when the threat of denied access to a grandchild is withdrawn. However, by whatever means it comes about, the issue of re-establishing position within the family is a common theme during the later phases of this work, once problematic drinking recedes. The client, now more aware of the effect that their drinking has had upon others, may wish to explain, make reparation or simply to build bridges. This may involve negotiating explicit agreements around alcohol.

For many clients, and particularly older people, who are more likely to have become isolated, the first opportunity to re-establish a sense of belonging can come through participating in groups. These could be groups specifically relating to alcohol, for instance relapse prevention groups, or could involve other activities which are broadly therapeutic in nature. Beyond this, clients may find companionship through activities such as local authority classes or in voluntary work.

NEEDS FOR ESTEEM

Low self-esteem is endemic in people who develop alcohol problems, and is almost always present by the time they seek help, when the recognition that they are dependent upon a substance such as alcohol has usually become a source of shame. The issues that lead to dependency and the effects of dependency itself are both likely to erode self-esteem and confidence. In addition, at the time when alcohol is first acknowledged to be a problem, people have often lost any sense of their own potential or faith in their ability to express it. This in turn frequently becomes a source of guilt, particularly if the difficulties caused by alcohol are contextualised by earlier periods of fulfilment or high achievement. Conversely the reversal of this process, the opportunity to rediscover and demonstrate one's worth to oneself through achievement, perhaps via planned goal setting, can be a valuable aspect of recovery.

Shame and guilt are potent enemies of self-esteem, all the more so because they are often borne in private. Gershan Kaufman, in *The Psychology of Shame*, makes the following point:

> Shame generally has been viewed…as visual and public. In contrast, guilt traditionally has been viewed as auditory and private. This assumption, which is fundamental to formulations of personality and culture, is in error because shame can be an entirely internal experience with no one else present.(Kaufman 1993, p.6)

Becoming able to speak about matters which have caused guilt or shame can be profoundly cathartic. The opportunity to share feelings relating to issues or events which may have been concealed for a long period of time, sometimes since childhood, can provide a great sense of relief, especially if the counsellor is able to act as a benign and non-judgemental witness. The release of pressure that often follows can act as a catalyst to begin the process of liberation from dependency, as it is very common for people to use alcohol to suppress unpleasant feelings, sometimes over a long period of time. When the need to do this is taken away the dependency is likely to diminish.

By enabling the client to speak freely the counsellor also facilitates the emergence of shameful or guilt-ridden experience into what might effectively represent, to the client, a public arena, albeit one containing only one other person and circumscribed by the safety of confidentiality agreements. For therapists who practise Rogers' Core Conditions (Rogers 1980) the maintenance of unconditional positive regard, an attitude that evidences belief in the client's intrinsic value as a person, can in turn allow the client to learn to experience themselves as a person of worth. It is common for people from this client group to question whether they are deserving of the support of family and friends, as well as professionals who may be involved in their care. An attitude on the part of the counsellor that consistently demonstrates a sense of the client's value can do much to alleviate this uncertainty and can also facilitate the development of rapport and trust. The process of learning to speak more openly and being valued by another can also form a precedent for acts of reparation towards people who have been affected by the client's drinking, thus compounding the sense of healing as relationships are repaired and re-established. Conversely by overcoming an alcohol problem a client sometimes discovers that the support of friends and family has never been lost: a very tangible demonstration of constancy and valuing.

Another factor that may contribute to lowered self-esteem is the erosive effect that alcohol can have on personal discipline and self-management skills. People with alcohol problems may have lost trust in their ability to maintain effective relationships, to hold down a job or simply to place resolve into action. This is another reason why helping clients to recognise and meet physiological needs can be so valuable: to establish good routines regarding diet, exercise and rest requires not only self-awareness but discipline and an ability to recognise a need and respond to it in an organised way. In practice this is often an incremental process, with each successful step contributing to an increase in confidence and therefore self-esteem.

There are also physiological reasons why an alcohol dependency can contribute to lowered self-esteem. Alcohol depresses the central nervous system, tending to result in lowered mood, which in turn can affect the way one views oneself (Blood Alcohol Information 2010). Additionally, a person who is frequently in a state of recovery as a result of binges or consistently heavy drinking may have little energy left for activities that might increase wellbeing and self-esteem. Much of the inertia that characterises people with alcohol problems can derive from simple tiredness, poor nutrition and lack of vitality.

This fact exemplifies the relationship between lower and higher needs: attending to physiological needs enhances the possibility of feeling better about oneself psychologically and emotionally.

While the use of alcohol is widely regarded as socially acceptable, the effects of problem drinking are often heavily stigmatised. Older people can be particularly sensitive to social stigma; an attitude that can contribute to the likelihood of social isolation if the drinker avoids company to hide their problem. One not uncommon scenario in this regard is when access to grandchildren is denied or restricted. Because most families now depend upon two incomes, grandparents often find themselves in the role of daytime carer. To be told by a son or daughter that this is no longer deemed safe because of their drinking can be a most humiliating experience, but one that can act as a powerful incentive to address the alcohol problem that has caused it. Shame can motivate. In addition, for the practitioner, being a witness to the restoration and healing of relationships that have been damaged by problem drinking can be one of the most rewarding aspects of working with this client group.

SELF-ACTUALISATION NEEDS

Self-actualisation could be defined as an intrinsic capacity and need for personal growth and an innate drive to maximise and express one's abilities. Maslow's (1954) description of the self-actualising personality was complex and multi-faceted. A self-actualised person would possess many attributes, including:

- realism, rather than being denying or avoidant of reality

- spontaneity

- creativity

- an ability to solve problems

- excellence in interpersonal relationships

- appreciation of life and experience

- autonomy: an ability to evaluate situations, make independent decisions and act on them

- objectivity

- a clear sense of identity, which may include a sense of vocation in the secular sense of the word.

Thus the process of self-actualisation involves both recognition and commitment to the ongoing expression of one's fullest potential. In the context of working with problematic drinking this may appear a tall order, as by their very nature people who develop an alcohol dependency are less likely to be self-reliant and self-determining than those who do not. However, it is important to realise that this theory, like Roger's Actualising Tendency, postulates that the capacity and need for growth is an *inherent* aspect of the human condition, and that difficulties arise when the process of growth is disrupted (Rogers 1961).

This perspective, if accepted, places both the causes of problem drinking and the potential for solution in a new light. It would be difficult to underestimate the challenge facing many people with serious alcohol problems to *imagine* a life without addiction, let alone one characterised by fulfilment and self-expression. The concept of self-actualisation suggests that such a possibility is actually natural. Many clients rue opportunities missed or situations marred through drinking. They may also speculate about other more favourable outcomes – what might have been. How then might a therapist begin to enable a client to first regain a sense of their potential and then begin to express it? Older people, and especially those with alcohol problems, are rarely thought of as having potential and, as suggested earlier, may initially be surprised to be viewed in this way.

Once again a clue might lie in asking what need lies behind the alcohol. For instance, for a client who is bored and lonely, what range of potentials does the opportunity to develop a stimulating social life contain? For a client with low self-esteem, what transformation might result from discovering confidence in their talents and uniqueness? For someone who is chaotic and disorganised, what possibilities might the development of self-management skills hold?

Older clients who confront these issues often do so in the context of limited life expectancy. Sometimes this in itself becomes a motivating factor: to stop drinking to make the most of what time remains, or indeed to extend it through improved health and wellbeing. At other times the sense of finite time remaining can lessen a client's resolve, and the dilemma of whether it is worth making a substantial effort to change in the face of what is deemed to be the likelihood of limited return must be addressed. Ultimately this question can only be resolved by the person facing it.

Underlying an exploration of the above possibilities is an onus upon the therapist to work with the client to develop a sense of their own potential. This can derive from what is learned from the client and should not be held rigidly as it must allow for continual redefinition as the client's capacity for change evolves. Two questions might helpfully be held in mind:

1.   What is the client's most natural way of being in the world?

2.   How can this be expressed?

Implicit in the concept of self-actualisation is the belief that individual fulfilment and development will naturally tend to benefit others, and indeed that the desire to develop oneself will eventually lead to a desire to offer skills, knowledge and other attributes to others in some form of service. An example of this is the fact that in several cases clients gave unsolicited permission to use their experience of counselling in the case studies that feature in this book. In every other case the request was consented to with little or no hesitation. This is worth mentioning because it is common for people with alcohol problems to believe that their dependency is evidence of their own selfishness, when clearly in many instances this is not the case. Therefore the prospect of concentrating on their own needs in therapy, though necessary, can initially compound their perception of themselves as selfish and self-centred. The counsellor may often hear: 'Someone else must need this more than I do.' Of course this must be challenged for the work to progress.

Herein lies the paradox of self-actualisation, and especially in relation to alcohol. It is necessary for clients to concern themselves with their own needs, particularly during the first phases of the work; however, in doing so they almost invariably become more self-aware, more aware of the needs of others and also less dependent upon others to meet their needs. An obvious practical example of this principle is that when people cease to drink problematically they typically need less medical attention.

Creativity is a salient attribute of the self-actualised personality and counsellors working in the field of alcohol will often meet creative people. Some, for instance, may exhibit creativity through their work or when pursuing interests, others may simply have a naturally imaginative way of approaching day-to-day life. Therapeutic work in the field of alcohol is always concerned with boundaries and people who are very creative often display noticeably different boundary systems. Maslow (1954) suggests that self-actualisation is accompanied by greater openness to life and experience. Hence people who are creative tend to be receptive in a way that is conducive to the influx of new ideas and inspiration. Because of this they are often more porous and more prone to being affected by their environment, including involuntary absorption of the thoughts and feelings of others. Such people often use alcohol both to inspire creativity and to close it down when they need to switch off. They will benefit if they are able to develop greater clarity of purpose and a firmer sense of personal identity, both attributes Maslow ascribed to the self-actualising personality.

SUMMARY

Underlying this model is the imperative to create propitious circumstances, including a facilitative inner environment, in order to equip the client to make whatever changes are needed: to create the right conditions to thrive without alcohol. The sequence in which needs might be met will derive partly from their perceived importance to the individual client and partly from the impact they are having on day-to-day wellbeing. For instance it is not uncommon to encounter highly creative people who are neglectful of their physical needs. This does not always detract from their creativity, but may have an adverse effect on their health. There are also those whose need for exploration or excitement, with any attendant risk, will outweigh the need for high levels of safety. Such clients might be more likely to relapse through boredom or under stimulation than the effects of a life in which chance plays a considerable part.

Finally it should be said that this model will not work for everyone, although aspects of it can almost always be applied usefully when developing a planned approach to the needs of individual clients. It will sometimes be the case that a client will be unable to define or articulate the need behind the alcohol or, having identified it, will lack the wherewithal to fulfil it. Occasionally prolonged alcohol misuse can permanently impair the ability to develop such necessary attunement. Where this is the case the client may still benefit from simple strategies to address the physiological and, if possible, social aspects of dependency. Nevertheless any movement towards the development of a capacity for personal fulfilment, which in Maslow's schema will tend to connect the individual meaningfully with others, will inevitably lessen dependency upon alcohol.

8

DETOXIFICATION (DETOX)

In this chapter we will describe in simple terms what detoxification is and what forms are commonly available. We will explain when and why detoxification might be advisable. We will also describe the place that detoxification has within the counselling process and the counsellor's role with regard to referral and aftercare.

Detoxification, often abbreviated to 'detox', is now increasingly referred to as 'medically assisted withdrawal' by clinicians and alcohol workers, perhaps to distinguish the process of clearing the system of alcohol from the more populist use of the term 'detox', meaning a dietary or fasting process involving a general cleansing of bodily toxins with the aim of enhanced wellbeing. In this chapter we will retain the abbreviation, with the understanding that it represents the process of assisted withdrawal from alcohol.

The process of detox usually involves the provision of a package of medical and psychological support over a defined period of time to enable a client to stop drinking. It is normally offered on the basis that the person undertaking it will attempt to remain abstinent when the process is complete. It is designed to help people who are unable to stop drinking of their own accord or who might be at medical risk in attempting to do so.

WHEN IS DETOX NECESSARY?

The following factors indicate that detox is likely to be necessary:

- *When it has been established that there is a physiological dependency*: A client shows evidence of a physiological dependency when they are unable to refrain from drinking without incurring significant withdrawal symptoms. These may include trembling, perspiring, headaches and anxiety or panic.

- *When a client is using alcohol to alleviate symptoms stemming from previous recent alcohol misuse*: Effectively this is a form of self-medication. The client drinks to try to ease the symptoms described above and in doing so compounds their dependency.

- *When there is a history of continual heavy drinking*: Where this is the case the client's system is never fully clear of alcohol. It is inadvisable for this sort of drinker to stop abruptly. If they are unable to achieve a stepped reduction detox will offer the best opportunity to begin the process of abstinence. Continuous heavy drinking includes regular daily drinking that is confined to one part of the day. The main feature of this type of drinking with relevance to the need for detox is that it allows no time for natural recovery from the toxic effects of alcohol.

- *When binges are of sufficient frequency, intensity or duration to make it dangerous to stop without medical support*: Heavy binge drinking is dangerous and can take a great physical and psychological toll. It is not uncommon for serious binges to end in hospitalisation. Drinkers who relapse following a period of abstinence often enter a binge, whether or not they displayed this pattern previously.

- *When for any reason it would be medically inadvisable for a client to try to stop of their own accord*: A high proportion of elderly drinkers will be physically frail, have medical conditions or be taking a substantial amount of medication. In the latter instance medication may need to be rebalanced when the system is clear of alcohol.

The type of detox that is offered to a client will ultimately be a medical decision made by a doctor or specialist alcohol nurse. However, it is helpful for counsellors to be aware of how such decisions are made because:

- they will be more able to direct a client towards the right level of treatment and to advocate for the client where necessary when referring

- through understanding when detox is advisable they will be unlikely to encourage a client to reduce or stop drinking in a way that would be medically inappropriate

- through gaining a basic understanding of the medical processes involved in detox the counsellor will be able to explain contra-indications between alcohol and the medications that are prescribed during and after the process.

THERE ARE THREE MAIN CONTEXTS IN WHICH CLIENTS RECEIVE DETOX

Home/community detox

Usually carried out by a doctor in general practice or specialist alcohol nurse. Normally the client will remain at home but visit the practitioner or agency carrying out the detox on a daily basis. The initial process normally lasts for about a week with subsequent follow-up visits to monitor progress and adjust medication where necessary.

Residential detox or rehab

Typically takes place over a period of several weeks in the premises of the agency offering detox. The actual detox is carried out in the first week. After this clients may receive intensive support in several areas including one-to-one keyworking, group work, medical support and dietary help/advice. The term rehab normally represents a more extended form of residential treatment which often includes individual and group psychotherapy and usually requires specific medical referral.

Hospital detox

Advisable when the client requires additional medical support. May also take place when the client is admitted for other medical procedures, through Accident and Emergency, or where a client with a mental health problem who also has an alcohol problem is admitted under the Mental Health Act 2007 (Department of Health 2009).

WHICH TYPE OF DETOX IS ADVISABLE?

The following is intended as a guideline only. It is important that counsellors seek advice where there is doubt about medical issues.

Home/community detox

May be appropriate for clients:

- who do not have a serious medical condition

- who have support, for instance someone to accompany them to the premises where detox will take place and to be with them at home during the process of withdrawal

- where there is no risk of alcohol-related seizure

- where there is no cognitive impairment or mental health problem causing confusion which might, for instance, prevent them from attending as necessary or complying with medication.

Residential detox

May be appropriate for clients:

- for whom home/community detox has proved unsuccessful

- whose home environment is not conducive to abstinence

- who need additional psychological support

- who need a longer period of time to consolidate abstinence before returning home.

Hospital detox

May be appropriate for clients:

- who have complex medical needs

- who are taking several types of medication or high doses of medication

- who would struggle to comply with detox medication unless supervised

- who have significant cognitive impairment or mental health problems.

As a potential route to abstinence, detox is only effective for clients who drink regularly. In general, clients who binge occasionally or at more regularly spaced intervals will only benefit from detox as an aid to recovery from severe episodes of bingeing. This is because binge drinking, by its nature, usually involves self-imposed periods of abstinence between binges. These may take place either as a result of the need for recovery or because the client binges in response to patterns of events, thoughts or feelings, with gaps between when no drinking occurs. This principle also applies to chaotic clients who binge sporadically with no obvious triggers. Although this type of bingeing can often result in the need for medical intervention which includes detox, the treatment in itself rarely creates a precedent for future abstinence.

A higher proportion of older people may require hospital detoxification because they are more likely to have serious health conditions or to be taking large amounts of medication. Older people may also have a lower threshold than younger drinkers because their systems are less able to process alcohol efficiently. For these reasons it is not appropriate to suggest exact levels of consumption as an indicator for the need for detox, rather the need will be indicated by a combination of the factors so far described.

THE COUNSELLOR'S ROLE

Preparing for detox

In the context of the counselling relationship the suggestion of referral into detox can be regarded as an important therapeutic intervention. Where the client's drinking patterns indicate that it might be appropriate, it can be helpful for the counsellor to hold the possibility of detox in mind from the time that counselling begins. Like any intervention, timing can be extremely important. Where there is no serious medical risk it can be valuable to allow the client time to reduce or stop without medical assistance. When working non-directively this may involve staying with any ambivalence that the client feels towards their relationship with alcohol generally, and also the issue of whether to aim for reduction or abstinence. This phase of the work may progress slowly. Many clients love alcohol even while recognising the harm it has done them. Clients may also become despondent regarding their perceived lack of progress at this time. When well timed, the introduction of the opportunity that detox represents can bring fresh hope. It is of course important that the offer to refer stems from an honest appraisal of the client's need, rather than impatience on the part of the counsellor. However, clients frequently come to welcome the possibility of medical assistance where their own efforts to stop drinking have proved unsuccessful.

When the client has agreed, detox has been arranged and a date is known, optimal preparation would involve negotiating a staged reduction in drinking prior to the event taking place. Where this is possible the client will experience less strain on their system and fewer withdrawal symptoms. Often, of course, it is not. Clients may even drink more than usual to compensate for the deprivation that the prospect of abstinence may represent at this point.

It is also very useful to begin to consider implications with regard to the changes in lifestyle that abstinence might involve, as clients often find these hard to envisage. What will they do during the times of day they have previously spent drinking? It is worth mentioning that for clients whose drinking has become ritualised, in other words is linked with other activities and conforms to a pattern such as regular evening drinking, the process of detox can effectively offer a hiatus in which another ritual can be introduced to supercede that which has been previously associated with drinking. Some clients, however, particularly those with regular daily habits, may benefit from preserving the rituals that surrounded their drinking. Others might feel that these will need to be abandoned, as they are too closely associated to the desire to drink and the activity of drinking itself. Here it is useful to explore options that might compensate for the likelihood that they will experience a sense of loss or disorientation. It is well worth encouraging the client, as far as possible, to imagine ahead and plan accordingly, and to make suggestions based on strategies that have worked for previous clients (see Chapter 9, 'After the Drinking Ceases/ Working with Relapse').

Another factor at this time is the trepidation that clients frequently feel with regard to the effects of the detox process and towards the prospect of abstinence. Both can be frightening and hard to imagine, and the client may benefit from both practical and emotional support. It is always worth explaining as clearly as possible what the process is likely to involve and emphasising that it will be carried out by an experienced professional or professionals. In the case of community detox we suggest discussing details such as how the client will reach the premises where the detox will take place and what support they will have before and after. It is also good practice to offer the option of providing phone support during the process for isolated or nervous clients.

Aftercare/relapse prevention

As mentioned above the detox process should ideally include both medical and psychological support. It is very important that the counsellor arranges to see the client as soon as possible after the process is completed to help to avoid the possibility of relapse, as clients often feel very vulnerable in the immediate aftermath. They may also feel confused or disoriented, experience strong cravings or physical symptoms such as headaches or digestive problems (see Chapter 9, 'After the Drinking Ceases/Working with Relapse'). Although in the context of this chapter the experience of detox is represented as a continuation of previous counselling work, it may also involve meeting the client for the first time, in cases where referral from another source has taken place once detox is completed.

Medication

When meeting a client who has just undergone detox it is helpful to be aware of medications that have been prescribed as part of the detox as the needs these are intended to meet are likely to influence the counselling process. The following are types of medication that might be prescribed during and/or after detox:

- *Medicines which help to reduce craving ('anti-craving')*: These are typically prescribed for a year to 18 months after detox. There is some risk of relapse at the point when clients stop taking them.

- *Medicines which act as a deterrent to drinking*: These are designed to produce unpleasant side effects such as flushing, vomiting, palpitations and headache if combined with alcohol. This type of medication is normally prescribed to clients who have had significant previous difficulty in maintaining abstinence. Clients taking this sort of prescription may experience particular frustration at their inability to drink. They may also experience conflict regarding whether to remain compliant.

- *Medicines which help prevent withdrawal*: Dosage is normally reduced as detox proceeds. Because one typical effect of this type of medication is to reduce anxiety it is important to be aware that anxiety may return or increase when the client stops taking it. Clients may benefit from learning skills such as relaxation as an alternative or complementary way of coping.

- *Vitamins, particularly vitamin B1*: An important aspect of clients' physical and mental recovery. In extreme cases vitamin deficiency caused by alcohol use can result in cognitive impairment. In its early stages this can be stabilised or even partially reversed through good nutrition (see Chapter 12, 'Dementia and Alcohol').

As with all medication, clients who experience significant side effects should be advised to consult their doctor. Counselling may also involve working with issues relating to willingness or ability to comply with prescribed medication.

The following are two examples of how the need for detox might arise within the counselling process:

Hamish was in his early 70s when I first met him. He had been happily married for many years and had children and grandchildren to whom he was close. He continued to run a successful company with an international profile, but changes in technology were beginning to make aspects of his business obsolete. Therefore he was faced with the dilemma of whether to continue in the light of diminishing returns or to relinquish an endeavour that represented much of his life's work. An ethical man and a conscientious employer, he was also very aware of the uncertainty that this situation caused his staff.

As Hamish was quick to point out, because he ran his own company no one could tell him what to do. This enabled him each morning to place eight to ten cans of beer on one side of his desk and move them across to the other side once empty. He believed that he had grown to drink so much in recent years because of the stresses of work. Doubtless this was a factor, but it soon became clear that he loved alcohol, despite coming to deplore many of its effects.

He had been born and brought up in an area of Britain where heavy social drinking among men was an established part of the culture, representing, he felt, a communal affirmation of masculinity. This custom had transferred to his later working life where the sales conferences to which he travelled around the world to conduct business dealings were invariably accompanied by heavy drinking. Alcohol had become a symbol of endeavour, creativity and reward. Therefore any changes in his drinking habits would inevitably have considerable impact on this aspect of his life and on his sense of himself as a person.

Hamish possessed great natural vitality and, doubtless, an innately strong constitution. He was also humorous and humane and displayed formidable mental acuity. These qualities however were unable to disguise that fact that the cumulative effects of his drinking had taken a severe toll on his health. As well as other minor ailments, he suffered from polymyalgia rheumatica, atrial fibrillation, type 2 diabetes, and had had two valves replaced in his heart. For these conditions he took 12 separate forms of medication.

Hamish described himself as an atheist and regarded himself as a realist: 'You can't control what happens to you but you can control how you respond to it.' He estimated that he might have eight years left to live and that 'it would be foolish not to make the most of them'. He suffered low self-esteem, further reduced by the decline in the fortunes of his business. He was an immensely cultured man who valued personal autonomy and had come to realise that many of the figures he admired in science, art and politics had been independent-minded individualists who also drank heavily. Despite this affiliation, and although he had been drinking heavily for most of his adulthood, he now believed that his life would contain greater choice and freedom without alcohol.

Two years before we met he had been able to stop drinking for seven months following a detox in a local hospital, with the subsequent support of relapse prevention and mindfulness groups at a local statutory alcohol agency (who upon learning that he was drinking again had referred him to me). After this period, which in the context of his recent history represented a considerable success, he attempted to begin a new life of moderate drinking, but with the pressures of work his consumption soon escalated back to its previous high levels.

We formulated an initial plan influenced by two significant factors: first, Hamish had a very supportive and involved GP, and second, detoxification could be a harsh and debilitating experience considering his physical condition and medical history. With this in mind we agreed to try a programme of very gradual reduction, monitoring progress at Hamish's suggestion by the use of a drink diary. If this proved even partially successful we would have the opportunity to review and decide whether to continue, or to apply for a detox, which in the event of a significant reduction in his drinking could be hoped to place less strain on his system.

Hamish was serious in his intent and enjoyed some sporadic success, but after two months, and despite his best efforts, we both felt that he would require additional help and that another hospital detox would offer the best chance of beginning the process of maintaining abstinence.

Arranging this involved negotiating two obstacles. Experience suggests that it can be more difficult for older people to access hospital detox, particularly those such as Hamish with a prolonged history of alcohol misuse and relapse. With this in mind and with his permission I contacted both his GP and a consultant psychiatrist from the agency that had previously treated him, both of whom proved willing to write letters of support. Despite their powerful advocacy there was some initial doubt regarding whether he would be deemed eligible. When this difficulty was overcome, Hamish himself felt that he had to delay his admission to attend to pressing work commitments. This stance was probably influenced by a variety of issues: his genuine anxiety over the future of his company, a possibly unconscious desire to postpone the moment when alcohol would be relinquished, the difficulty of imagining a future without alcohol, and perhaps an understandable reluctance to undergo a stressful and emotionally loaded medical procedure.

Eventually, some five months after his decision to ask for a detox, he was admitted to hospital for a week, after which our meetings resumed. Hamish was surprised at the physical impact of this procedure, which proved greater than those he had previously undergone. His medications had been adjusted and he felt drowsy and irritable and was experiencing regular cravings. As is typical with people with long histories of alcohol misuse, Hamish had seemed disassociated from his physical needs; however, in the absence of alcohol the debilitating effects of his medical conditions came to the fore, as did issues relating to his self-esteem. Despite this he managed to remain abstinent for three months and then, as before, began to drink occasionally.

Significantly, although his consumption rose again it did not return to previous levels, no doubt helped by his decision finally to relinquish his business. When reflecting upon our work, every step of which had been driven by his own choices, he felt that it had enabled him to stabilise his drinking.

When we first met, Wendy was in her mid 70s and had been drinking heavily for over 30 years. She was a practising artist and teacher of art, whose stated discipline was to work at this chosen vocation for several hours of each day. A cultured person with a down to earth manner, she had a well-developed aesthetic sense that included a love of gourmet food and wine. She was a highly accomplished cook and hostess and took pride in presenting themed dinner parties, of which a choice of fine wine was an integral part.

Since losing her husband 20 years previously she had lived alone, with the company in recent years of a beloved budgerigar, with which she spent each evening, following an identical routine. At a regular time she would prepare food for herself and snacks for her budgie and they would eat together while she watched television. These meals were always accompanied by red wine and Wendy invariably drank more than she intended. She hoped to learn to restrict her consumption to one or two glasses each evening, but feared she lacked the willpower.

In recent years Wendy had suffered from a variety of ailments, including a serious heart problem, which had resulted in a period of hospitalisation, and which coincided with the unexpected death of a younger relative to whom she had been very close. This experience had left her depressed and traumatised, and she felt guilty at having been the one to survive. She spoke of a persistent sense of futility and said she could find little enjoyment in pursuing former activities such as visiting galleries.

Despite this she still worked at her art and continued to teach students in her home, finding in this long-held practice a temporary relief from depression. In fact during the course of our work it became clear that the practice of art and the experience of depression were somehow antithetical. Although she often struggled to begin work each day, once underway the creative process always lifted her into a different mindset. Like many people who suffer depression, Wendy realised that she found respite in disciplined activity, and her art also offered self-expression and a meaningful and compelling way to engage with the world.

Although Wendy had been drinking for a long time, her drinking pattern was very contained. As already described it invariably accompanied meals and usually took place between set hours in the evening. Furthermore she was very selective in what she drank, both in the type of drink and in the quality. I pointed out that these factors showed that she was already applying self-imposed boundaries around her drinking, a very positive indication for our work.

As mentioned, Wendy had hoped initially to cut down rather than stop entirely. I thought this was a realistic aim, as a contained and selective pattern of drinking is probably the most amenable to controlled reduction. However, she was not confident. Although she often drank alone, serving and sharing alcohol was an integral part of the way she entertained her friends, and she was proud of her hospitality and of her role as hostess. She feared that by portraying herself as a non-drinker she would somehow lose face. Also, as a young art student, her initiation into social drinking had been associated with romanticism, rebellion and a burgeoning sense of the world of aesthetic appreciation. In contrast, alcohol had also become a way of coping with her innate sensitivity. At times she felt exhausted and powerless and drank, alone, 'to feel numb'.

We met each week, and for three months she tried to reduce but, despite much discussion, struggled to define clear targets and therefore to be consistent in her intent, a vital element in controlled drinking. Indeed she now wondered whether her best hope was to try to stop completely. During this phase of our work she held a successful art exhibition as a result of which her drinking temporarily escalated to a bottle of red wine a day, a dangerous amount given the fragile state of her health. At this point I suggested the advisability of detox, saying honestly that I could see no evidence that she was able to reduce in a structured way, and hence to learn to drink moderately. I also said that I thought she would probably find abstinence easier to accomplish, because as an aspiration it represents an unequivocal statement of intent, allowing none of the grey areas that can accompany controlled drinking. Of course these grey areas multiply once alcohol has been consumed.

Disappointed and frustrated with her own efforts, Wendy agreed to be detoxed, although she felt much trepidation about what the process would involve. I sought to clarify this. With her permission I contacted a local statutory agency with a staff of medics and paramedics and made enquiries on her behalf. Because of her medical condition and the amount of medication she was taking there was some discussion as to whether she would need to be hospitalised. She was offered an appointment in which these and other factors were assessed and it was deemed safe to offer her a community detox in which she would attend the agency's premises for an hour each morning for a week. She was advised to arrange for a friend to accompany her each day and to stay in her home until the process was complete. Immediately after this our work would resume, effectively becoming aftercare at that point, and we arranged to meet at the beginning of the week following her discharge.

In our last meeting before her detox began, Wendy expressed even greater nervousness at the now imminent prospect. She feared failure: 'I know I will be annoyed with myself if that happens.' She remembered displaying intolerance to members of her family who had struggled to give up cigarettes or recreational drugs, and now realised that she felt just as harshly towards herself in her own kindred situation. Despite these feelings, and ever practical, she had arranged to spend each evening of the detox week with a variety of friends, in a determined attempt to disrupt the ritualised patterns of behaviour that had become so entwined with alcohol.

When we next met she had completed the detox successfully, but not without difficulty. Thanks to the expertise of those treating her she had suffered only mild physical withdrawal symptoms. However, deprived of the comfort of her routine, and perhaps the sedative effect of alcohol, she had experienced anxiety attacks upon waking each morning, also prior to the only evening she had spent alone. Because of their severity I took her through a 25-minute relaxation exercise, which we repeated in subsequent weeks and which she also practised at home. Alcohol can act as a shield to unassimilated events and feelings, and I reassured her that this sort of traumatic experience, though very unpleasant, is usually transitory, also that she would almost certainly be better able to develop insight into its causes now that she had stopped drinking.

Wendy proved able to remain abstinent, but there were many adjustments to make. At first her dreams became more vivid and were sometimes disturbing. She was more than usually affected by the suffering of others when she watched the news. She became very aware of the sense of impermanence that had accompanied the simultaneous events of her illness and bereavement. She also became aware of a habit of procrastination that displeased and frustrated her, also that fear deriving from a sense of insecurity had somehow turned her into a hoarder, and her home was full of unwanted detritus.

We continued to work with these and other issues for another six months. During this time she developed a renewed clarity and confidence with regard to her art and teaching and, despite the temporary intrusion of a brief but debilitating illness, was able to hold another exhibition. She continued to host dinner parties and to serve wine to her guests. The latter events remained an important aspect of her social life, and also contributed to her self-esteem and sense of identity, factors that counterbalanced the obvious risk involved.

When the time came to end our meetings her morning panics had ceased and her health had improved. She still missed alcohol and felt that she would probably always do so, but her loss was mitigated by the aspects of her lifestyle she was able to retain and by pride in the considerable achievement that being able to stop drinking represented.

9

AFTER THE DRINKING CEASES/WORKING WITH RELAPSE

'Alcohol was my companion, my lover, my true friend.'

In this chapter we explore the processes involved in relapse prevention. This includes working with the initial after effects of withdrawal, helping the client to acknowledge and process emotions that have been hidden by alcohol use, re-evaluating, reframing and rebuilding relationships and creating new behavioural precedents. We also explore the significance of relapse as an indicator of triggers for drinking and relapse as an aspect of the therapeutic process.

THE INITIAL STAGE OF ABSTINENCE

Almost all clients who aspire to complete abstinence will require further support once drinking stops. This is particularly true of clients with complex needs and/or an extensive history of problematic drinking, for whom relapse prevention is likely to represent a substantial proportion of the counselling work. As a rule of thumb, the amount of support needed to consolidate abstinence will be proportional to the severity and duration of problematic drinking prior to cessation. This phase, which may in its entirety encompass recovery, self-healing, review of relationships and the exploration of new possibilities, can require substantial commitment and stamina on the part of the counsellor, although it can also be very rewarding.

For long term problem drinkers, the act of learning to live without alcohol can best be characterised as a transitional process that will affect every area of life. Clients who have been drinking for a long time are likely to feel that they are entering new territory when they begin to try to live without alcohol. At the outset it might prove difficult to appraise realistically the challenges that abstinence presents, and indeed these will vary considerably for each individual.

The period immediately after cessation tends to contain some common characteristics, with clients reporting similar experiences, although again there will be much individual variation. Clients might find that they are challenged to adapt physiologically, psychologically and socially. Previous habits that were formed around drinking or influenced by drinking will need to be reviewed, and perhaps adapted or discarded. The following are common experiences when drinking stops.

Insomnia

Alcohol is a sedative, and although it adversely affects sleep quality clients often struggle initially to sleep without it. It can take several months for sleep patterns to normalise and clients frequently report debility due to poor sleep in the intervening period. If this becomes overly problematic the client should be encouraged to consult their doctor.

Vivid and often troubling dreams

Alcohol suppresses the rapid eye movement phases of sleep that are associated with dreaming (Roehrs and Roth 2001). During the initial period of abstinence dreams may become, or seem by comparison, particularly vivid and/or disturbing. It is reasonable to speculate that this phenomenon may also be influenced by the re-emergence of issues that have remained unprocessed because of alcohol misuse. Problematic drinkers commonly use alcohol to suppress unwanted thoughts and feelings.

Mood swings

Alcohol is often used to enhance pleasure and to dull pain. In its absence the client may become far more aware of changes in mood, and might be tempted to revert to drinking in an attempt to regulate feelings that are no longer masked by alcohol. People who develop alcohol problems tend to be particularly intolerant of lowered mood states. The counsellor will frequently hear: 'I drank to cheer myself up' or 'I drank to try to forget about it'.

Craving for sweet things

Alcohol contains a great deal of sugar. In the initial stage of abstinence it is common for clients to develop a sweet tooth, to compensate for the immediate loss. If they are able to adopt a good diet, and thereby learn to regulate their blood sugar levels, this phase is normally transitory.

Poor appetite

Many problem drinkers neglect to eat well. Some in the latter stages of an illness may not eat at all. In addition alcohol damages enzymes in the gut that play an important part in good digestion. Aversion to food is quite common, particularly after detox, and where possible the client should be encouraged to eat little and often. Again this phase is normally transitory. If it persists the client should be encouraged to consult a doctor.

Flashbacks

Clients frequently report the re-emergence of powerful and evocative memories, particularly if they have experienced any form of trauma. This may be because alcohol has been used, consciously or otherwise, to suppress memories and difficult emotions. The saying 'I drink to forget' has passed into common usage. Alcohol can also adversely affect memory as a cognitive function and so its absence may allow new access to past events.

Unrealistic optimism

Some clients feel markedly better after the first week, during which the initial physiological effects of withdrawal will normally have passed. Because of this they may fail to be aware of the need for continued vigilance until the habit of abstinence is established. This may particularly be the case for clients with bipolar tendencies (noticeable mood swings) who sometimes experience transitory elation when their system is clear of alcohol and thus free of its attendant depressive effect.

PRACTICAL CONSIDERATIONS

For the counsellor the initial stage of abstinence can represent a very practical phase of the work in which clients may be encouraged to attend to basic needs such as rest, nutrition and rehydration. There may be much confusion and anxiety in relation to the newness of this experience and many clients benefit from learning relaxation and breathing skills at this time. If the counsellor is able to model self care and calmness this will also be extremely valuable.

Ideally this early phase will also mark the start of a transition from self-neglect to a new habit of self care. The development of self-awareness is often a particular theme during this period and much of the counselling work will involve helping the client to become conscious of past patterns that link with their drinking. It is important to realise that long term drinkers may have had a variety of motivations for drinking, and hence that their relationship with alcohol might have changed and become more complex over a period of time.

Clients may feel particularly vulnerable while first learning to be abstinent. They also may feel weak and unwell because of the effects of their former lifestyle and the after effects of detox, where this has taken place. It is most important to be sensitive to the possibility of fragility and confusion and to proceed tentatively, offering support rather than challenge, as illustrated by the following case study:

When Geraldine, nearly 60 and currently living alone, arrived for her initial assessment her skin was noticeably yellow and her manner suspicious and uneasy. She had spent the previous five weeks in hospital and had emerged with a diagnosis of liver damage involving cirrhosis and hepatitis. In addition she had been diagnosed with jaundice and malnutrition and in the recent past had also suffered pneumonia. In the month immediately prior to admission she had drunk brandy throughout the day and even at points during the night and had ceased to eat. A consultant at the department of hepatology had advised her that she would not live until Christmas, at that point nine months away, unless she stopped drinking. And she was determined to stop: 'I have Hobson's choice.'

Because of her physical weakness a dietician had advised her to eat as much as possible, but the thought of food repelled her. She also strongly associated meals with alcohol. We explored the possibility of eating little and often, concentrating on foods she found appetising, and fortunately she was still able to enjoy fruit. I also encouraged her to drink water regularly and to rest whenever she needed to.

Geraldine was very concerned that I might pry into her past and so I asked her to tell me if she found anything I said too intrusive, and promised to respect her wish for privacy if she indicated that any area we touched upon proved too sensitive. We agreed to meet weekly.

During the next six weeks she began to relax somewhat and to speak with increasing candour about her current situation and the events that had led to it. Her recent time in hospital reminded her of the sense of restriction and abandonment she had felt during a week spent in a children's ward when she was five. 'In those days they [parents] weren't allowed to stay.' The feeling of abandonment had grown stronger when her father died a year later. In our third session she brought a picture of a mother with a baby, in a cosy room with open french windows showing a view into the distance. She said this imagery symbolised for her a combination of constancy and freedom, and we returned to these themes throughout the 18 months in which we met.

CONSOLIDATION – RELAPSE PREVENTION

Ideally the term relapse prevention represents a holistic process that will equip the client with the skills, insight and stability to live without alcohol. Once again, the principle of learning to meet needs via means which do not involve drinking is paramount, and many factors relating to this aspect of avoiding relapse were covered in Chapter 7, 'Addressing the Problem: Alcohol and the Hierarchy of Needs'.

If a substantial amount of work has taken place prior to abstinence, it may have been possible to identify clearly some of the thoughts, feelings and/or situations that led to problematic drinking. This information will provide forewarning of likely triggers for relapse. If however the client is already attempting to be abstinent at the time of the first session, for instance after detoxification, it might be helpful to ask the following questions:

- Where there was a history of relapse during previous attempts to be abstinent, what factors preceded each occasion of relapse?

- Is there any pattern of relapse? (e.g. does it coincide with dates relating to significant events such as divorce or bereavement, is it likely to happen at weekends or on certain days of the week? Is it cyclical and driven by fluctuating moods, or is it apparently random?)

- Is relapse more likely to occur in specific circumstances? (e.g. in certain company or social situations, or when the client feels pressured by others, or lonely or isolated?)

- Can relapse be linked with certain emotions, or an identifiable pattern of feelings, or with psychological states such as depression or anxiety?

- If so, can these be linked to events or activities that might in themselves be regarded as triggers?

It is also important to establish whether the client is experiencing craving for alcohol. If so:

- at what level? (mild/moderate/intense)

- how frequently does it happen?

- does it increase at certain times of the day or in certain situations?

For further information please see Chapter 6, 'Working with Types and Patterns of Drinking'.

By making this sort of enquiry both client and counsellor can begin to develop a more precise picture of the significance of alcohol in the client's life. The counsellor is also likely to learn much about the client's personality and personal history. Where relapse follows a pattern or corresponds to specific events it can be helpful to develop individually designed coping strategies. Examples might include:

- exploring social possibilities with isolated clients for whom loneliness has been a factor in their drinking

- reframing behaviour at mealtimes that were habitually associated with alcohol. This might for instance involve negotiating with others where meals are shared or substituting a non-alcoholic drink to preserve a sense of comfort where solitary drinking has become ritualised

- practising how to refuse alcohol. This can be particularly valuable in situations that are traditionally associated with alcohol such as weddings, christenings, funerals and Christmas gatherings

- exploring ways of re-educating acquaintances who have habitually associated the client with alcohol. This will involve learning to present in public as a non-drinker.

It cannot be overemphasised that clients do not always anticipate problematic situations and so can often benefit from prompting on occasions when the counsellor is able to anticipate scenarios that could lead to relapse. It can be very helpful to rehearse with the client how they might cope with a known or even hypothetical situation. This sort of preparation can both instil confidence and prevent the client from being taken by surprise. It is also important to attune to the particular needs of each client as triggers for relapse can be very individual. A contingency that might be easily managed by one client could prove challenging or overwhelming for another. Having said this it is always worth preparing with the client for emotive occasions that are culturally linked to alcohol, for instance Christmas, weddings, funerals or christenings. Where anniversaries of bereavements are known preparation is also advisable. Continuing with the case study:

During the first few weeks in which we met Geraldine spoke with concern about symptoms of stomach pain, diarrhoea and nausea, and wondered: 'Are these psychosomatic?' I suggested she should seek advice from her GP, following which a series of endoscopies revealed some benign polyps in her gut, which some months later were removed. Despite this her appetite gradually returned and for several weeks she developed a habit of eating trifle or cream cake and coffee at 2 am: 'instead of my brandy'. This led us to explore an aspect of craving: 'Moderation – I've never been able to do it. Also a brandy lasts an hour – a cream cake lasts two minutes.' I suggested that by making this substitution she had discovered an effective way of coping with a situation that might otherwise have led to relapse, as she was aware of the craving and able to respond to it without using alcohol. I also suggested that as a strategy it might be amenable to further adaptation. We explored the need behind her actions: 'It's comfort eating – it stops me getting stressed', and discussed the possibility of learning to satisfy the need before it grew into a craving, an aspect of which would involve eating small nutritious meals regularly throughout the day. Geraldine gradually was able to adapt to this pattern, which she came to enjoy, and after two months her dietician advised her that her weight was exactly right for her height and build. And she still had the occasional cream cake for a treat.

In the sixth session she remembered the disorientation she had experienced when she entered hospital: 'During the first week I didn't know where I was.' She also began to experience panic attacks when away from her home, which paradoxically seemed to be exacerbated by her gradual return to health: 'I've got energy again – it's a pain!' In one instance she went on a coastal walk: 'I got to a point where I couldn't go forward and couldn't go back – in the past that's when I'd have had brandy.' Fortunately on this occasion the feeling had soon passed and I explained that panic attacks, unlike anxiety, are transitory and hence, although frightening and unpleasant, are by their nature short lived. As a response, we agreed to allocate 20 minutes in each of the next three sessions to relaxation and breathing exercises, and I said that thereafter she could ask for them if and when she felt she needed them. The idea behind this was threefold: to help her to reduce her residual levels of anxiety, to enable her to develop skills that she could apply in times of distress, and to encourage her to attune to her fluctuating moods and learn to respond to them without resorting to drinking, thereby diminishing their power.

Because Geraldine described her renewed energy levels as something of a problem, and because despite her drinking she had always been busy and active, we reviewed the current structure of her week. With her doctor's agreement she was attending exercise classes twice per week; she had also resumed her former habit of visiting the theatre or cinema each month with a group of friends, all of whom still drank quite heavily. In addition she had signed on to an agency for part-time work in child care, a field in which she had much experience.

We explored the balance between her need for activity and stimulation and her need for rest as part of her continuing recuperation, mindful that both boredom and tiredness can be potent triggers for relapse. She decided to re-enter the world of work tentatively, accepting no more than two days of agency work per week. Although her energy levels were increasing, she had become more aware of times when she felt tired, currently most days after lunch. In the past she would have taken brandy to allow her to carry on; now, with some encouragement from me, she decided to take an afternoon nap.

WHEN RELAPSE OCCURS

The occurrence of relapse in clients who aspire to abstinence is frequently an integral part of the counselling process and may best be viewed as an opportunity for developing greater understanding of the client's relationship with alcohol. It can be seen from the above that the situations and contingencies that involve the possibility of relapse can help to clarify triggers for drinking and so can be viewed as a valuable aspect of the therapeutic process. Therefore, if relapse occurs, it is useful to be aware of gradations and specifics within the experience, for instance:

- relapse during which drinking does not escalate to its former level

- the drinker who relapses but does not go on to binge, where previously they would have done so

- longer periods between relapse

- decrease in number of triggers for relapse

- relapse which involves only one type of drink, where before selection of drinks would have been indiscriminate

- situations in which the drinker manages to increase the period between the impulse to drink and the act of yielding to it. This is particularly helpful for binge drinkers, who are typically impulsive.

All of these scenarios point to the likelihood that the client is beginning to exert some influence over their drinking. Relapse can also provide further insight into the client's relationship with alcohol if the counsellor and client explore the following factors:

- changes in patterns or triggers for relapse

- identifying new or different reasons for relapse – what has changed? What can be learned?

- strategies for preventing the accumulation of anxiety, where this has been a factor

- exploring ways of coping with depression, where this has been a factor, or encouraging the client to seek medical help if the depression is ongoing or severe (see Chapter 13, 'Depression and Alcohol')

- exploring 'fallback positions' that do not include alcohol

- exploring any signs of an emergence of a new sense of self – helping the client to imagine and begin to actualise a future and identity without alcohol.

Although in many cases clients will notify that they have relapsed, the counsellor will not always have forewarning. In many cases the client will simply not attend. Where this happens it is very important for the counsellor to try to maintain contact by letter or phone. This will help the client, who may well be feeling ashamed and despondent, to re-engage in counselling as soon as possible. If there are extreme concerns regarding the client's wellbeing and safety it is also very important to notify other carers/healthcare professionals who are involved with the client. Ideally an agreement relating to this possibility will have been made during initial contracting, in which the client will have been given the opportunity to nominate someone whom they would trust in such a circumstance. Where concerns relate to health or serious risk of harm it is also advisable to contact the client's GP, and again it is preferable to seek permission for this possibility at the outset of the work.

If the counsellor is working for an alcohol agency it is likely that they will have formulated a protocol regarding relapse. For instance, if the client is temporarily unable to attend because of relapse or its after effects, they may be required to contact within an agreed period or risk having their case closed and hence a delay in the resumption of counselling. The primary therapeutic aim of a measure such as this is to try to maintain continuity in the work, also to encourage the client both to take responsibility and to express their need for help. Clients should be given every opportunity to re-engage and protocols should never be presented as punitive.

BEYOND RELAPSE PREVENTION

The needs of people with an extensive history of alcohol misuse can rarely be met satisfactorily through short term therapeutic interventions. Long term work (i.e. counselling of at least one year's duration) is usually necessary for the client to develop the confidence and skills to consolidate the initial phase of abstinence. A longer time frame can allow the counselling relationship both to deepen and broaden. It may deepen in the sense of becoming more psychodynamic: when trust in the relationship and the client's self-confidence with regard to maintaining abstinence has developed the client may wish, and feel better able, to look more deeply into painful events from the past, with a view to finding understanding, healing or closure. It may broaden by encompassing the exploration and stimulation of interests, desires and aspirations that represent a new or renewed sense of potential, and hence a more hopeful future.

Alcohol can mask or stunt the ability to grow and develop, and genuine personal fulfilment is rarely accompanied by the feeling of deficit that invariably co-exists with an alcohol dependency.

This phase of the work might feel more spacious, as the client's initial fear and sense of urgency dispels. As it progresses it is increasingly likely to involve helping the client to acknowledge and process emotions that have been hidden by alcohol use.

The re-emergence of powerful feelings, only some of which may seem to stem from current events, is frequently a salient characteristic of this time. Clients often say that they do not know where such feelings come from, as they do not appear to have been triggered by any recognisable current experience, or perhaps represent a disproportionate response to a seemingly trivial incident. It would seem from the vivid, disconcerting and often transitory nature of these reactions that they may be amplified by, or perhaps be wholly attributable to, past emotions and experiences that have not been processed because of alcohol misuse, but are now coming to the fore. This is further evidenced by the fact that they are so often accompanied by psychosomatic phenomena, for instance sudden sweats or stomach cramps which pass as quickly as they came.

As uncomfortable as these experiences can be they are likely to be short lived and their emergence, however unpleasant, can indicate that the work is gathering momentum now that the suppressive effect of alcohol has been removed. It cannot be stressed strongly enough that clients who learn to process their feelings are less likely to relapse, and that feelings cannot be processed unless one is aware of them. The sense of movement that the increasing ability to process represents is the antithesis of the emotional and psychological inertia that so often accompanies alcohol misuse. To continue with the case study:

By the 12th session Geraldine had been able to talk about two family members who had died as a result of heavy drinking. One death was very recent and its circumstances reminded her of her own former denial of her alcohol problem. She was very saddened that she had found help but the relative in question had not. In addition to this for several weeks she had experienced random times of sadness and weeping, without having a clear sense of any cause. She was also becoming frustrated at the need to attend hospital regularly for checkups and minor procedures, and said that she was beginning to feel controlled by healthcare professionals, especially as she had been advised that she should not yet return to work, an instruction she had ignored.

As we explored these issues Geraldine said that she was starting to develop a clearer idea of who she really was: a person who was essentially independent, energetic and free-spirited. She was also increasingly aware of the damping effect that alcohol had had on these characteristics. She expressed a strong desire to take control of her life. I noticed that she was far more open and expressive now, also that she was using the time in between sessions to reflect and develop upon the themes and issues we discussed.

LEAVING ALCOHOL BEHIND – THE EMERGENCE OF A NEW SENSE OF SELF

As confidence in the ability to live without alcohol grows, the need to discuss it explicitly usually lessens, and it is natural to shift towards an exploration of a future beyond a life that has been dominated by alcohol, and indeed a life beyond counselling, or at least counselling in which the main focus is alcohol. Therefore if alcohol is mentioned less now it is unlikely to be because of avoidance, as it might have been in earlier sessions.

This time, which represents the final phase of consolidation, might involve encouraging any inclination the client shows to try new things or different approaches and so accept the challenge of pursuing a more fulfilling life. It can be of great value if the counsellor is able to work with the client to develop and maintain a sense of their innate self and potential and to explore how these might be most naturally expressed in their day-to-day life. Older people, and particularly those with alcohol problems, are rarely viewed in this way and yet the absence of alcohol, combined with many years of lived experience, can provide fertile ground for a late flowering of self-fulfilment through personal development, relationship and the desire and ability to contribute to life. Any counsellor working with this client group is likely to be struck by the many and diverse qualities of the people they encounter, many of whom will relish the renewed opportunities that improved health and self-confidence can bring as the influence of alcohol dependency recedes.

When clients begin to imagine and voice new possibilities it can indicate a need to re-engage with more practical aspects of the work. There is much therapeutic value in nurturing the confidence to place resolve into action. Any client who has remained abstinent for a significant period of time has already demonstrated significant ability to do this. In addition people with alcohol dependencies often exhibit both tenacity and resourcefulness over periods of years in maintaining a drink habit alongside their family, work and social commitments. These qualities can be acknowledged and redirected to new purpose. Typical themes from this time may include:

- *Clearing away*: A further letting go of ideas and attitudes that are now recognised as unhelpful or perhaps obsolete. This activity is frequently accompanied by a physical correlate in the form of clearing accumulations of clutter. Both make space for new possibilities. A useful question can be: 'Should I keep it, adapt it or discard it?'

- *Re-evaluating, reframing and rebuilding relationships*: Also perhaps letting some go. When an individual stops drinking it inevitably has a ripple effect on those around them. There may be work to do in helping the client to enable others to see them differently. Sometimes relationships are transformed; others, especially those based primarily around alcohol, may not survive the process of dis-identifying with the harmful effects of a former shared lifestyle. The client may also feel the need to apologise or make acts of reparation for past behaviour, now seen in a different light.

- *Re-socialising*: Clients who have become isolated and wish not to be may need help to make contacts. It is useful to keep information on activities or centres available in the area, or to offer to refer the client to a person or agency with specialist knowledge of these.

- *Problem solving*: Nurturing the ability to tackle rather than defer problems. This is another aspect of processing and may include empowering the client to access and ask for help. If throughout the work the client has been encouraged to review and express their needs, for instance in deciding the frequency of sessions, it will serve as a useful precedent.

- *Regret*: Clients may express regret for past behaviour or missed opportunities. Most poignant perhaps is the regret for wasted years and 'the person I might have been'. The ability to voice this regret can do much to alleviate the sense of shame and alienation that so frequently accompanies alcohol misuse.

- *Self-expression*: Clients may have 'found their voice' in terms of speaking more confidently and authentically; counselling can be particularly helpful in this respect. They may also have found or returned to interests that provide a channel for self-expression such as music, writing or painting which may all enhance the ability to process feelings.

- *The emergence of a new sense of identity*: Clients often contrast their former self with 'the person I have become since I stopped drinking'. They may feel able to see themselves with renewed clarity and to feel 'more comfortable in my own skin'.

- *Support systems*: Many older people are vulnerable and will have ongoing needs beyond counselling. Such clients will benefit from a discussion regarding referral to services that can offer further appropriate support such as medical help, financial advice, advocacy or befriending. Evaluation forms we have received from clients also suggest that a significant number do not feel confident that alcohol has ceased to be a problem despite prolonged abstinence and the apparent success of counselling. This concern is likely to be eased if they feel well supported in other areas of potential need.

By acknowledging and working with these themes the counsellor will do much to mitigate against the likelihood of relapse.

A final point: People who develop an alcohol dependency will often display high levels of dependency in other areas of their lives. Dependency is by no means always problematic: the desire to place trust and reliance upon others is intrinsic to the human condition, as interdependency is intrinsic to meaningful relationship. However it is very likely that clients will have derived particular security from the counselling relationship and hence may experience considerable trepidation as its end approaches. It is valuable to acknowledge and explore such fears as they may contain the final seeds of the potential to relapse. We will say more on this in Chapter 10, 'Endings'.

As our relationship deepened Geraldine spoke more about her sense of abandonment: 'Everybody leaves.' As well as the family members referred to earlier her husband and later a long term partner had died. She had grieved, but she believed that her drinking had disrupted the momentum of her grieving, leaving it incomplete, and now she expressed her unresolved sorrow. She also reflected on the death of her father, which had occurred when she was six. She had come to realise that the irritability and remoteness he displayed towards her was almost certainly a result of the illness that preceded his death. It now seemed to her that when he died her mother was somehow given freedom, and that this freedom was passed to her. She remembered long days spent in the fields near her home with her friends and her dog. As an adult she had travelled whenever the opportunity arose, and she saw in her young self the dawning of this expansiveness of spirit. She had observed in the course of her child care work that 'children are able to go further from their carer when they feel safe', and remembered the security she had felt in knowing that her mother would be waiting at home.

Further to this theme of abandonment I had noticed that she had maintained a sizeable number of loyal friendships, all of which seemed to have survived her transition into abstinence. Some were sensitive and encouraging. One friend suggested going on a day trip on Geraldine's birthday, where previously they would have visited a restaurant and drunk heavily with their meal. The group with whom she visited the theatre and cinema, long established drinking companions, also willingly accepted her new choice, although she admitted to finding their company less fulfilling without the stimulus to camaraderie provided by alcohol.

Not everything was easy. A friend with whom she visited a race meeting each year drank twice as much as usual. Geraldine's comment: 'He was drinking for both of us,' says much about the systemic nature of co-dependent alcohol misuse. Geraldine also saw in his conduct a reflection of her own former behaviour when drunk, which she now found boorish and incompatible with meaningful relationship.

She also noticed changes in the attitude of her family towards her, enjoying a new authority amongst her siblings, who began to turn to her for advice, doubtless in recognition of her innate strength and capability.

She found herself able to endure with greater equanimity the invasive medical procedures that she still had to undergo as her health continued to be monitored: 'I've come a long way.' She was also able to be more assertive when dealing with medical people, where previously she had viewed herself as a passive victim. Nevertheless she regretted times when, unable to contain anxiety and frustration born of illness and loss of autonomy, she had been rude and childish towards hospital staff.

During the first four months in which we met Geraldine had experienced bloating and stomach cramps, which she believed were caused by the anti-craving medication she was advised to take. I was aware that this was a known side effect and suggested that she should discuss the matter with her GP. Because in the absence of this treatment craving can return abruptly, and hence provoke relapse, we reviewed the strategies she had developed to counter times when she longed for alcohol. Early on, Geraldine had made a deliberate decision not to avoid situations involving alcohol: 'It's been too great a part of my life.' Further, on her own initiative she had decided to walk along, rather than around, supermarket aisles stocked with alcohol, feeling that she needed to be able to cope with the day-to-day exposure that is part of contemporary life. She therefore felt confident that she could cope without medication, and so it proved. In addition her digestion improved, as she had hoped.

Other changes came about. Tests had revealed that Geraldine was anaemic. As she had been taking iron tablets this was thought to be due to malabsorption, caused by the damaging effect of alcohol upon the stomach lining. Geraldine was sensitive towards the tiredness that resulted and, although fearing that she might appear selfish, would sometimes leave social gatherings early to respect her ongoing need for rest. A person with great natural drive and vivacity, she was learning to pace herself.

After six months she was beginning to feel established in her new way of life – she was not going back. Now accepting regular part-time agency work and in a new relationship, she had gained the confidence to resume taking short trips abroad from which she returned refreshed and stimulated. The richness and scope of possibility that her life now contained made a poignant contrast to what she now saw as many wasted years, and for a short time she grieved for the self that might have been. She wondered whether to explore these regrets or 'put them in a box', and decided to 'look then move on'. This short but evocative phase allowed her to acknowledge her sense of loss, but in so doing recognise more clearly her many qualities, not least of which were practicality and a zest for life. Without minimising her sadness she decided to look forward and conceived the idea of taking a three-month working holiday in the USA to study organic farming methods, which she hoped to apply to her allotment, which increasingly occupied her spare time.

While she waited for a visa, at her request, we returned once again to some unresolved aspects of her life when still drinking. She was keen to understand why, in the light of her new self-recognition and understanding, former interests and activities had born so little fruit. Surprisingly in view of her commitment to our counselling work, it transpired that she had never been able to persevere: 'I never stayed anywhere.' She felt that this stemmed partly from impatience, perhaps a manifestation of the desire for instant gratification that often accompanies alcohol dependency, but also from a deep-seated lack of confidence. She gave an example of attending an evening class in which she had been easily deflected from the aim of learning basic sewing skills because she had felt inferior to more advanced students, an attitude that now seemed remote, particularly as in retrospect she was able to recognise how willing her fellow students had been to help her. More confident in her own independence, she believed she was now less likely to exclude the kindly interest of others.

Geraldine did visit America. As well as learning much and feeling at home in a country which she felt contained a wealth of possibility, she worked for two weeks in a vineyard and visited the place where a famous bourbon was manufactured, as if to honour the romanticism that still attached to many of her experiences involving alcohol. We met once more on her return, by which time she had taken a full-time job and clearly had no further need to see me. The following Christmas she sent me a picture of the elderflower cordial with which she intended to celebrate the festivities.

10

ENDINGS

In this chapter we will explore what is meant by a 'good ending'. We will describe types of endings and look at the particular challenges of ending well and appropriately with this client group. We will also explore the subject of dependency in relation to ending and the question of how to end with clients who have ongoing needs.

WHAT IS A GOOD ENDING?

Every counselling modality recognises that it is important to end the work and the counselling relationship well, where this is possible. But what does ending well mean? An ideal scenario might involve acknowledging that the end is imminent, before addressing any unfinished business, reviewing the relationship and whatever changes it has encompassed, and finally spending some time looking to the future beyond counselling. Also implicit in the concept of a good ending is a sense of completeness on the part of both client and counsellor. Again from an ideal perspective this might derive from a belief that the client's presenting issues have been addressed satisfactorily, which in turn might mean that they have resolved or are no longer experienced as problematic, or that the client feels they have gained sufficient resources to continue to address them without further support. This happy state of affairs is most likely to come about where there is an opportunity to agree the timing of a natural ending, which may not be possible for a variety of reasons, but particularly if the work must take place within a defined period of time or number of sessions. In discussing the process of ending we will assume that the counselling contract allows adequate time to address the issues of older clients presenting with a long term history of alcohol misuse and other related needs.

Inevitably, when working with clients who may have been drinking problematically for anything up to 50 years, the subject of recognising when it is time to end and implementing a good ending becomes more complex. Superficially this might not appear to be the case, because success or failure in alcohol counselling is inevitably measured in more objective terms than can usually be applied within general counselling. This is because, whatever subsidiary benefits might be involved, a successful outcome is primarily defined in terms of whatever behavioural change has occurred with regard to the client's drinking. Therefore, if the client has achieved their nominated goal of reduction or abstinence and maintained this for a period of time, the work could be deemed successful and therefore complete.

Several factors mitigate against this supposition. Older people who have experienced alcohol problems, and particularly those who have been drinking problematically for long periods, may have ongoing care or support needs in relation to such matters as health, mobility and finance, as well as the potential to become isolated. They are also more likely to continue to experience loss in a variety of forms. These factors make them more vulnerable to relapse, and it is important to take this into account, where the time frame in which one is working allows, when deciding the point at which the work will end. For this reason, as mentioned earlier, we advocate the value of longer term work, which allows the client to consolidate upon initial progress and which permits client and counsellor to make a thorough holistic exploration of the client's needs in relation to overcoming their problem with alcohol. We know from feedback gained via evaluation forms given when the work is finished that a significant proportion of clients who wish to remain abstinent still experience trepidation regarding their ongoing ability to do so. This can be the case even for those who have been abstinent for an appreciable period of time and who have made significant improvements in other areas of their lives.

In addition, even if the client does appear confident, how does the counsellor know that confidence is not misplaced? For instance binge drinkers, and particularly those who experience significant mood swings, often cannot imagine the possibility of relapse until it happens, because they are unable to access the feelings or moods that accompany relapse until they are actually experiencing them. Other types of drinkers may also be unrealistic and wish to end prematurely. Sometimes this might stem from a lack of experience in relation to abstinence or controlled drinking; at other times it can result from false optimism that may occur when the depressive effect of alcohol is removed.

For all of these reasons it is important to hold in mind that the client might be vulnerable to relapse when counselling ends, and indeed that the prospect of ending can precipitate relapse if it is not timed correctly, or if the factors that caused the client's problem with alcohol are not fully addressed.

TYPES OF ENDINGS

It is possible to divide endings to pieces of alcohol counselling work arbitrarily into three categories:

1. Those that arise 'organically' because both counsellor and client feel that the work has achieved its aims and is therefore complete.

2. Those that come about because there is an agreed time limit or imposed limit to the number of sessions available to attempt to complete the work.

3. Those that end prematurely because the client drops out, or chooses not to continue while still drinking problematically.

As we have already suggested, we believe that it is preferable for the client and counsellor to be able to decide together the right or natural time to end. We take this view for a variety of reasons:

• It is congruent with a non-directive approach in that it encourages the client to sense from within the point at which they are ready to end.

• It allows the client to choose to relinquish the support that the counselling relationship has offered, thereby affirming their autonomy.

- It represents a final affirmation of mutuality within the counselling relationship in that the client's perception of their needs continues to be respected as the work closes.

- It allows the counsellor to 'adjust' the timing of the ending in the light of any contingency that suggests the client might benefit from further support, thereby ensuring that the client has time to resolve any issues that emerge during the latter part of the work which might otherwise lead to relapse.

We recognise, however, that there is an increasing requirement for counsellors employed by both statutory and non-statutory alcohol agencies to complete the counselling work within a defined period of time or number of sessions. Counsellors working in private practice might also be constrained by the number of sessions a client is able to afford. In some instances this will limit the scope of the work, although it may have the benefit of increasing the intensity of focus upon the problem at hand.

If the duration is limited to a set number of sessions one viable way to prepare for ending can be to reduce gradually the frequency of sessions in the latter part of the work. This has the benefit of increasing the time span in which counsellor and client meet. It also gives the client the opportunity to demonstrate to themselves that they are able to cope without the support of counselling for increasingly greater lengths of time. When this is implemented successfully sessions preceding the ending can typically assume the character of a 'check in', in itself a sign of decreasing need for support.

When ending time-limited work it is particularly important to summarise and review salient issues in relation to the client's drinking, with an emphasis on identifying any outstanding needs and/or triggers for drinking. Often these coincide, and when this is the case referral into other forms of support can be particularly valuable. For instance, clients for whom boredom has been a trigger can benefit greatly from structured activities, while those who drank because of loneliness or isolation are far less likely to relapse if they can be introduced to meaningful social opportunities.

Sometimes it is not possible to complete the work, and counselling work with this client group can end prematurely for a variety of reasons. On some occasions this can be by mutual agreement, for instance if the client finds an alternative source of help, or if it is decided for any reason that they are unable to benefit from counselling. Circumstances such as illness or relocation to another area may also dictate the need to end. In some instances, however, clients simply drop out. Where a client fails to attend without notification, and then fails to respond to initial attempts by the counsellor to sustain contact, the counsellor is left with a dilemma regarding what further action to take. In some cases there may be guidance deriving from policies and protocols in the workplace. Agreements might also have been made regarding contacting a third party in certain contingencies, usually if there is concern about the client's safety, and we recommend that specific arrangements should be negotiated at the time of assessment where possible (see Chapter 5, 'First Session/Assessment'). An additional complication is that at this stage it is not possible to know whether the client's absence represents the final end or simply a hiatus in the work.

This scenario raises the question of duty of care in the light of legislation regarding Protection of Vulnerable Groups (HMSO 2006). Clearly not all older people who drink problematically will fall into this category; however, where there are serious concerns it is important to try to ascertain the client's safety, where this is possible. This might involve contacting their doctor, a carer or family member, or another healthcare professional who is involved in their care. In any such communication confidentiality should be preserved as far as possible, with information being shared on a need to know basis according to the policy of the organisation.

Another aspect of premature or unplanned endings is the likelihood that the counsellor will be left with unresolved feelings regarding the work and their relationship with the client. Even the most experienced and professional therapist may feel concern, bewilderment, frustration or even anger when a relationship in which they have invested much time, care and effort ends abruptly and without explanation. There may also be a sense of disappointment at relinquishing prematurely one's part in the client's story. If such feelings are not addressed they can accumulate, resulting in despondency, a sense of failure and eventually even burnout (see Chapter 11, 'Self Care and the Therapist'). Therefore it is very important to take any 'unfinished business' with regard to the counselling relationship and its apparent outcome to supervision, particularly as this type of ending is likely to be a recurrent theme in work with this client group. It is particularly natural to continue to have concern regarding the client's ongoing welfare, but also essential to balance this with a clear sense of the limits of one's responsibility. Supervision can do much to help process residual feelings and re-clarify boundaries and hence to retain a necessary level of objectivity towards the work.

ENDINGS AND THE 'DEPENDENT CLIENT'

Endings are inevitably coloured by all that has gone before them and, although the counsellor should always consider certain factors in terms of completing the work, they should not, as far as possible, be approached in a formulaic way. Rather they should relate to what has been learned during the counselling interaction as a whole, to the context of the client's personal history with particular reference to their relationship to alcohol, and to their future life in the light of whatever changes have occurred regarding their drinking. Of course they will also be influenced by the character and quality of the relationship developed between counsellor and client.

When considering endings with this client group one important factor to be aware of is whether at the time of ending the client retains any vestigial dependency towards the counsellor and/or the counselling relationship, and if so what implications this might have when the time comes to end. On the whole our experience suggests that dependency upon the relationship usually diminishes naturally if the client is able to reduce or eliminate their dependency upon alcohol. However, as might be expected even in the context of a non-directive approach, some clients may come to regard the counsellor as a guide or even mentor with regard to alcohol. To an extent this is a legitimate view. Counsellors working in this field are normally expected to acquire specialist knowledge as they are dealing with a specific subject matter. Although of course clients should be encouraged to discover their own expertise and wisdom regarding their relationship with alcohol there will be times when it is the place of the counsellor to give information or to intervene when, for instance, they are more aware of the possibility of relapse than the client. This aspect of alcohol counselling, the counsellor as 'safety net', can sometimes heighten any trepidation that the client may feel towards the prospect of ending. In particular, special care should be taken if the work has encompassed any issues relating to previous loss and abandonment. A 'tapered ending', in which the frequency of sessions is reduced gradually and with sensitivity towards clients' perception of their needs, can help clients to demonstrate to themselves in safe stages that their reliance on the counsellor is genuinely decreasing. As already suggested it can also do much to help clients anticipate the eventual possibility of continuing without specific support in relation to alcohol.

Contrary to popular belief, we see little evidence that people who develop an alcohol dependency are necessarily likely to develop dependencies in other areas of their lives. In some instances dependencies do become more generalised, resulting in, or from, the so-called 'dependent personality', but at other times they can be extraordinarily specific. To give two examples: the artist who drinks while he sculpts but would never consider doing so when painting, and the binge drinker who will only binge on one type of (good quality) alcohol. In addition, a significant number of clients that Mike has worked with have displayed reluctance to take more medication than they feel is strictly necessary for conditions such as anxiety, depression and insomnia, further negating this supposition.

Nevertheless, anyone who has sought counselling for an alcohol problem will have done so because they felt unable to resolve it alone. They will have experienced something of the helplessness that is an inevitable aspect of alcohol dependency and are therefore likely to doubt their future ability to cope without support. Some approaches, notably 12-step methods, have reinforced this tendency by encouraging the client to admit that they are 'powerless' in the face of their dependency, and will therefore always need support.

In contrast to this, our experience suggests that dependency upon the counselling relationship is, for many clients, a natural but essentially transitory aspect of successful alcohol counselling. It could also be argued that temporary reliance upon the counselling relationship is both inherently less harmful and qualitatively different from dependency upon alcohol, as by its very nature effective counselling, while offering support and constancy, seeks to stimulate the client's inner and outer resources, and thereby to maximise autonomy.

THE RELATIONSHIP BETWEEN REVIEWS AND ENDINGS

In a way the ending could be seen as the ultimate focus of the work, the desired result, the point of becoming. Often what the client hopes to achieve, and feels able to achieve, is defined and redefined, and therefore the end and its accompanying outcomes are reframed and re-imagined as the client seeks to develop a measured and realistic sense of confidence in their ability to gain ascendancy over alcohol.

Regular reviews offer the opportunity to recognise explicitly any diminishing need for support, and growing confidence, on the part of the client. This in itself can be regarded as an aspect of preparation for the eventual ending, as could acknowledging phases of change regarding the client's attitude towards alcohol and their relationship with it.

Another way to decrease any abruptness the client might experience in relation to ending is to treat the end of a piece of work as the final part of a process of reviewing the client's situation and progress. One aspect of initiating a process of regular reviews is that it creates more organic opportunities for the client to identify and address any unmet needs that could contribute to relapse. Clearly this is particularly valuable when the work is due to end, because it can help to indicate what other forms of support, if any, a client might need when counselling is no longer available. Again this is an important aspect of helping the client to meet needs through means that do not involve alcohol. Changes in the client's attitude and perspective might mean that they are more able to access help that was always there, for instance through supportive family or friends, but which had previously felt inaccessible because of the distancing effect of alcohol. Alternatively sometimes clients, and particularly those whose relationships revolved around drinking, may feel that they need to establish an entirely new network of friendship and support. Occasionally clients for whom alcohol appears to have ceased to be a problem will find that they have outstanding issues still to address, and may choose to seek additional counselling or equivalent support elsewhere. Clients may also continue to need support in relation to practical issues such as mobility, finance and health, all of which can contribute to the potential for isolation and the depression or anxiety that so often accompanies it.

However carefully the counsellor might plan and implement the ending it is never possible to be entirely sure that the client will not need further help at some time in the future. Counselling work involving alcohol is often characterised by a series of episodes, sometimes with spaces of several months or even years between each. Therefore a good ending might mean one in which the client can return for further help if it is needed, or perhaps feel able to seek help elsewhere. In cases where a client has broken off without notice it is important that some form of contact is made. If there is no reason to believe that they are at serious risk a letter inviting future contact may enable a client to return at a later date, or to feel able to seek help elsewhere.

11

SELF CARE AND THE THERAPIST

In this chapter we describe some particular challenges of working with this client group and explore ways of coping with them. We look at issues relating to counter-transference and empathy and list some practical measures to protect the counsellor's wellbeing. We also include at the end of the book exercises in mindfulness, relaxation and meditation that can be used in the counselling work or for the therapist's own benefit.

The activity of counselling can require considerable reserves of stamina and durability from the therapist. It can involve intense concentration, also the ability to combine genuine involvement in the relationship with sufficient detachment to maintain an overview of the counselling process as a whole, including a realistic sense of the client's ongoing needs and the part that counselling might play in meeting them.

Counsellors working with older people with alcohol problems are likely to encounter specific additional challenges. This client group will present with as broad and diverse a range of issues as could be expected to be encountered in general counselling; however, these will be augmented and intertwined with the ageing process and with alcohol dependency, the latter often making them more complex and inaccessible. As stated earlier, because they have lived longer it is likely that a higher proportion of clients will present with more extensive histories of drinking and alcohol-related problems, which will consequently be more entrenched and difficult to work with. There is also significantly greater likelihood of exposure to illness and the effects of illness than in general counselling, and additionally a higher proportion of clients are likely to present with issues of bereavement and loss. The counsellor will also meet more people who have, or have had, mental health problems, as people who suffer from mental health problems are more likely to develop an alcohol dependency than the general population (Institute of Alcohol Studies 2007b). In addition problematic drinking can exacerbate and complicate an existing mental health problem and reduce the likelihood of effective treatment (see Part III, 'Working with Complex Needs/Dual Diagnosis').

Working with these factors in combination can require much skill, patience and indeed optimism on the part of the therapist, particularly in the early stages of the work, in which the therapist often 'holds the hope' on behalf of demoralised clients who may have been battling dependency unsuccessfully for many years. As experience develops, particularly if it involves being able to witness positive outcomes that might initially have seemed improbable, this can become easier. Nevertheless the need to foster self-belief in the client, and the energy and faith that this calls for, will always be present at the beginning of the work and often beyond.

Self-neglect is endemic in people who develop serious alcohol problems, where lack of confidence, low self-esteem and poor health have eroded the desire or ability to attend to basic needs. In turn burnout, experienced as a combination of exhaustion, anxiety, flattened mood, loss of confidence and loss of trust in one's judgement, is prevalent in the field of counselling and psychotherapy and in the caring professions generally (Mateen and Dorji 2009). This combination of factors makes it additionally important not to underestimate the energetic impact of working with clients with an alcohol dependency. Both the potential for absorption of the client's emotional material and the additional energy required to work with people who are stuck or who tend towards inertia can take a heavy toll, particularly as the prevalence of psychological and emotional inertia in long term drinkers places a great onus upon the therapist to develop and maintain momentum in the work.

Therefore, for a variety of reasons, it is a useful discipline for the therapist to monitor counter-transference, and particularly any cumulative effect that is experienced as meaninglessness, lack of motivation and/or erosion of personal discipline or boundaries. One of the most important functions of supervision can be to assist in this process, and so help the therapist to recognise and address any tendency to absorb or be adversely influenced by these traits, which so characterise the client group.

The term vicarious traumatisation has been used to describe the accumulative effect of encountering the traumatic experiences of clients on a regular basis over a sustained period of time (Sexton 1999). Therapists, often those who are most empathic, can experience involuntary somatisation of their client's way of responding to experience. For example, therapists who work regularly with clients who experience panic and anxiety states might find themselves holding patterns of tension in their body which mirror the effects of panic or anxiety observed in or described by the client. This may occur either through the unconscious absorption of the client's reaction to fear or, conversely, as a result of guarding against such a possibility. Holding such patterns of tension can, by their nature, leave therapists themselves more vulnerable to feelings of panic and anxiety which, if not addressed, can accumulate. Additionally, in some instances, therapists might also find that they develop symptoms of illness or trauma resembling those of their clients. When considering these phenomena in terms of their somatic and energetic impact it is valuable to remain particularly aware of the most typical physical manifestation of empathy: mirrored body language.

When a therapist, or indeed anyone, attunes closely to another person in conversation there is often an involuntary assimilation and replication of the way that they sit, gesture and speak. This is widely seen as an asset in counselling training as it represents an overt demonstration of the ability to become involved in the world of another and hence to exhibit interest and empathy. For the very reason that this is a natural, and therefore usually unconscious phenomenon, it is important for the therapist to learn to be aware of it and to recognise that, however valuable, there are times when it is not appropriate. For instance if a client presents with pressure speech, agitated body language and shallow breathing it will benefit neither party if the counsellor is drawn into similar behaviour. At such times it is important to remind oneself of the need to retain one's own posture, breathing and sense of personal space and identity. Both client and counsellor will benefit from this, as the counsellor, although aware of the client's anxiety, is less likely to internalise it. In addition the client is given the opportunity to observe and draw from the calmness that the counsellor is modelling, and so begin to learn a different way of responding to fear and situations that induce fear.

It is therefore helpful to make a clear distinction between empathy and indiscriminate absorption in the context of the counselling relationship. A most valuable definition of empathy is: 'the ability to know fully the experience of the other without releasing within our own body the survival response of the sympathetic nervous system' (Cade and Blundell 1979, p.9). In other words, to understand without being overcome or making the client's problems and problematic responses one's own. Clearly this is not always easy, as it calls for a fluent combination of involvement and detachment – apparently polar opposites.

WHAT MIGHT HELP?

The following factors could all play a part in reducing the possibility of burnout and hence making the work more effective and less arduous, as well as safeguarding professional longevity.

Regular effective supervision

This will be vital in terms of helping the counsellor to process thoughts and feelings about the work, which in turn can provide useful modelling to a client group that typically struggles to do this in the initial stages. Supervision most valuably can also help to ensure the maintenance of personal and professional boundaries, always especially important in the field of alcohol misuse.

Personal therapy

All counsellors are obliged to have personal therapy as part of their training. Some choose to continue this practice as a valuable or necessary complementary activity to their client work. This is a matter of personal choice, based on one's own need and inclination. However, any activity that helps the therapist to process, heal and develop will sit well alongside one's own professional practice and will contribute to a more holistic and therefore more sustainable way of practising.

Developing the habit of reviewing sessions by monitoring counter-transference in energetic terms

For example, by asking:

- Have I gained or lost energy while I was with the client?

- How has the quality of my energy changed?

- What am I left with after a session?

- What do I do with it?

Developing the habit of reviewing sessions by monitoring counter-transference in terms of somatic impact

By asking:

- What physical feelings, tension or discomfort am I left with?

- What do I do with this?

- Can it be cleared?

General self-monitoring

It is particularly important for the therapist to be aware of changes in personal habits that might indicate the beginnings of self-neglect, for example less care in grooming and general appearance, hygiene, diet, exercise and, of course, increase in alcohol consumption. This will not only help to safeguard the therapist's own wellbeing but can also provide another form of valuable modelling for the client.

Training

Counsellors working with this client group will regularly encounter clients who are suffering from physical illness or pain, or who are concerned about medical issues and medication. Generic counselling training rarely addresses these matters explicitly and the counsellor might feel overwhelmed or out of their depth in terms of knowledge or understanding. In consequence it is advisable to seek specific training in working with these issues. It is also valuable where possible to have access to medical advice where the implications of illness may influence the content and outcome of the work.

Collaboration

It is important to remember that *you don't have to do it all yourself* and that other healthcare professionals either will be involved in the care of the client or can be approached to become so. It is likely that clients who have been referred by statutory services will already be part of a care plan and both client and counsellor can benefit from co-ordinated collaborative working (for the confidentiality arrangements that this might involve see Chapter 5, 'First Session/Assessment').

Activities that provide contrast

Counselling is an intense, sedentary activity that takes place indoors, usually in the confined space of a small room. Therapists may find balance from outdoor activities such as walking, running or cycling, or from swimming or gym work. Others might benefit from relaxing company, cultural events or solitude, or perhaps the respite from dialogue offered by periods of silence.

Relaxation, mindfulness and meditation

The ability to relax intentionally, the possibilities for self-awareness that accompany the practice of mindfulness, and the stillness and calm of meditation can all offer refreshment and, with practice, allow the possibility of responding differently to or recovering more quickly from stressful situations. In the Appendix are three simple exercises that can be practised with benefit by the counsellor and/or used as tools to offer clients.

Monitoring caseloads

What constitutes a realistic number of clients for a counsellor to work with at any one time depends on several factors, for example the complexity of individual cases, whether the therapist has other duties such as group work or keyworking, whether the work involves travel between premises, and the frequency of sessions for individual clients.

Size of caseload is not always within the therapist's control, although any professionally run service should ensure that staff members are not overloaded. It is important that therapists are able to discuss their workload on a regular basis with their line manager, or if in private practice to develop the habit of reviewing it regularly with their clinical supervisor.

Holidays

Regular holidays can prevent the build-up of tiredness and the accumulative psychological and emotional effect of carrying a large or exacting caseload of clients. The prospect of working towards a clearly defined break can also increase the ability to cope when current duties feel onerous. Taking steps to avoid the accumulation of tiredness will do much to prevent the possibility of burnout.

Humour

The ability to laugh and to find benign amusement within one's work is a valuable personal asset, a factor in maintaining morale within a team and a potentially useful therapeutic tool. As well as lifting the spirits it can help to maintain a sense of perspective.

SUMMARY

Sensitivity is a necessary quality in counselling; however, sensitive people are often the most porous and therefore most prone to burnout and compassion fatigue. Self-knowledge, the ability to monitor one's own process, appropriate professional support, and the willingness to involve others where necessary in the care of the client are all factors that can reduce the inherent stresses of working as a counsellor. They will also increase the ability to maintain a firm sense of one's own identity and hence reduce the risk of over-identification with individual clients and the client group. This is particularly true for therapists who have themselves previously struggled with any form of alcohol or substance misuse.

WHAT TO LOOK OUT FOR

The following signs might alert a counsellor to the need to take action:

- tiredness, particularly persistent tiredness

- feelings of apathy or despondency

- anxiety or panic

- feeling overloaded

- feeling unable to care about clients

- inability to 'hold' clients, i.e. a significant number of clients drop out or leave without explanation – concerns about this should be balanced by an understanding that because of the nature of the work it is not unusual for clients to drop out, often temporarily. However, a counsellor who has ongoing concerns about this issue should discuss it in supervision

- falling into the role of rescuer – this is a particular risk when working with vulnerable elders, where the client's potential to attain realistic levels of independence and autonomy is balanced against any ongoing need for support stemming from their personal, medical and psychological situation.

When I first met Mercedes, a respected and widely experienced counsellor and supervisor in full-time private practice, she had recently suffered an alcohol-related seizure brought on by 18 months of heavy drinking. She had undergone detoxification in hospital and in our first meeting expressed considerable fear of alcohol in view of its recent dramatic effect upon her life. A moderate drinker before this experience, she hoped never to drink again. However, she felt vulnerable and disoriented, and said explicitly that she needed to be held therapeutically.

Although during her initial sessions she struggled to maintain clear lines of thought, in part no doubt because of her seizure, Mercedes quickly revealed herself to be profoundly sensitive, imaginative and empathic. She also had great command of counselling theory, enhanced by her studies in anthropology. She favoured 'an egalitarian style of communication and way of being' and I imagined that in her practice, which was currently suspended due to her illness, she would be very skilled in building a respectful and trusting relationship with her clients. From subsequent discussions it became clear that she had been greatly in demand and had carried a large and complex caseload.

Mercedes told me that her drinking, and the depression that had accompanied it, represented a 'withdrawal from life'. I wondered if within this withdrawal there had been an element of seeking respite. Mercedes thought about this and said that it had offered a 'sort of disengagement', and that she tended to put others first.

Because she had worked as a therapist, and because she displayed so much self-awareness, I was keen to explore what support systems had been in place during the time that her drinking had become problematic. Mercedes believed in the value of personal therapy for the therapist, and had been in individual therapy when her drinking began to escalate; however, she found that there were 'no-go areas in relation to alcohol' with the therapist she was seeing, and she had felt unable to share fully this aspect of her experience. In addition, the long and fruitful relationship she had enjoyed with her supervisor had initially been disrupted when he became ill and later had ended when he died.

Another factor in her eventual misuse of alcohol, I felt, was Mercedes' exponential personal development in the context of her family history. Typical in this respect of many members of her generation, she was an only child of parents who had not had the opportunity to pursue further education. She had attended university and gained higher degrees, and this aspect of her experience was without precedent in her family. Thus she had to find her own limits in terms of role and achievement, and the struggle to limit her drinking could be seen as a metaphor for the need to manage limits in other areas of her life.

Mercedes was happily married to a loving and supportive husband, but during the time in which she became ill had felt lonely. Perhaps this related in part to the inherent loneliness of anyone who is in any way a groundbreaker. However, she described an existential loneliness that seemed to stem from her acute awareness of the human condition. At one point during the early part of our work she was intensely affected by a humanitarian disaster reported on the news.

Despite the range and scope of her achievements, Mercedes retained a profound sense of her own and others' humanity. A naturally open person, she believed that it is hard for therapists to show or express vulnerability without attracting stigma. She also believed that her success had invoked a jealous reaction from some colleagues in the profession, and felt that this had been a factor in her breakdown. As well, her status as a therapist and what it represented had made it difficult to acknowledge her problems with alcohol, and her current inability to work deprived her of much of her sense of identity. To balance this, she was grateful that a significant number of friends and colleagues had remained loyal and supportive.

Mercedes' use of language was rich, beautiful and full of nuance. She told stories about her life to illustrate her experiences. In doing this she created a sense of sharing. Early in the work her narratives tended to be circuitous, but always provided valuable information and insights. At this stage I found it helpful to summarise towards the end of each session. As the threat and effects of alcohol receded I became a privileged witness to the gradual return of her natural acuity, and with it confidence in the expression of her beliefs. Part of this process involved the reaffirmation of her core values as a therapist, which in turn helped to clarify how she wished to practise in future.

Week by week we developed further insight into the factors that led to her excessive drinking. Being the possessor of unusually high levels of empathy and sensitivity, though a gift in a therapist, made her more porous. Mercedes' caseload had included some particularly challenging clients. Alcohol had increased the tendency to absorb, at times indiscriminately, the emotional and psychic material she encountered, but had undermined her ability to process it effectively. Sensitive people have a greater need to process their experience regularly because their interaction with people and events leaves a deeper imprint. When this need is not met, thoughts and feelings can accumulate and become oppressive or overwhelming. In such circumstances alcohol can appear to offer respite from consciousness, from the task of being aware.

In relation to this, Mercedes was quite clear that depression preceded the escalation in her drinking. There had been personal factors: a significant bereavement in her family concurrent with a bout of illness and concerns about the wellbeing of other family members. She also recognised that she had overstretched herself, an insight that was illustrated by a dream of feeding children at her breast but being unable to satisfy them. The dream also exemplified the poignancy, for such a caring person, of her current inability to offer succour through her work.

Fortunately, because as a self-employed practitioner she could receive no sickness pay, her doctor had supported her in applying for benefits to give her time to recover, and after several months it was clear that her recovery was underway. She made frequent references to the loyalty she had attracted in this difficult time, and set about re-establishing a personal and professional support system, with increasing confidence that this would no longer be undermined by the distancing effect of alcohol. We acknowledged the onus upon counsellors who work in private practice to develop and maintain their own support systems.

She had come to feel that, like her father, she had given too much of herself, calling this trait 'careless love', and she determined to be measured in the way she returned to work, and to balance her caseload by choosing clients and supervisees carefully. She began to speak with greater professional authority during the sessions, acknowledging this implicitly by saying 'I must retain my self-directiveness – I had come to lose it.' A sense of once again being in touch with the needs of her body returned, 'literally being brought to my senses', and, as well as enjoying food, she began to attend a gym. She recognised the value of attending to her own development and fulfilment alongside that of her clients, saying: 'I must continue to be creative myself.' This thought reminded her of the approbation and encouragement she had received as a child from a neighbour, who despite having six of her own children, had shown her great love and attention. The memory of this kindness had become a formative influence in her practice as a therapist.

Towards the end of a session, after we had been meeting for about a year, I asked Mercedes what else she felt she needed. When she smiled and said 'I'm fine' we knew the work was complete.

PART III

WORKING WITH COMPLEX NEEDS/DUAL DIAGNOSIS

12

DEMENTIA AND ALCOHOL

*In this chapter we will explore the clinical, ethical and practical issues involved in working with people with dementia who also have an alcohol problem. We will describe the counsellor's role in relation to the client and also as part of co-ordinated treatment processes involving other healthcare professionals and carers.**

DUAL DIAGNOSIS

The term dual diagnosis normally describes people who combine alcohol or drug dependency with a diagnosed mental health problem. Such clients usually present with complex needs in terms of treatment, as each condition will interlink and therefore tend to exacerbate the other. In the context of therapeutic work involving an older client group we would like to include under this term people who have a combination of alcohol dependency and dementia, as there can be no doubt that problematic drinking will influence the progression and management of a dementia, also that dementia will complicate treatment of an alcohol dependency.

---

* Parts of this chapter have previously been published in the *Journal of Dementia Care* (Fox 2008) and are included with kind permission of Hawker Publications.

151

DEMENTIA AND THE COUNSELLOR'S ROLE

Dementia is a generic term for a group of illnesses whose salient characteristic is progressive cognitive impairment. The effects of dementia can cause considerable distress as well as practical difficulties for both the sufferer and those close to them. Until comparatively recently it was unlikely that people with dementia would be deemed able to benefit from counselling. However, in recent years this view has begun to be revised, leading to the emergence of services and individual counsellors who are finding innovative ways to offer effective emotional and psychological support to this client group.

The possibility of counselling people with dementia who also have alcohol problems may sound additionally daunting, but our experience encourages us to believe that a field of treatment can be developed to offer such people meaningful help.

From the perspective of the counsellor who works with older people with alcohol problems it is perhaps useful to divide cognitively impaired clients into two categories:

1. Those who have received a formal diagnosis of a dementia.

2. Those who exhibit behaviours consistent with some form of cognitive impairment which may not have been diagnosed, or in some cases even recognised, at the time of referral.

Each will require an individual approach designed to meet their specific combination of needs. However, a particular challenge when working with the latter group is the need to distinguish whether presenting characteristics such as confusion and memory loss are attributable to dementia, to alcohol misuse, or to a combination of both, also whether they are temporary or permanent. Counsellors working with clients who present in this way may be able to perform the following important roles:

- encouraging clients with apparent memory loss or confusion to contact their doctor to be referred for specialist diagnosis

- helping clients either to abstain or reduce consumption to minimal levels, to enable clinicians to make an accurate diagnosis of their condition

- offering similar help to clients who would benefit from anti-dementia medication but whose levels of alcohol consumption preclude safe prescription.

Problematic drinking can prevent accurate diagnosis. In our experience clinicians in memory services prefer clients to be free or nearly free of alcohol for a two-month period before testing for dementia. Also, because alcohol is contra-indicated with anti-dementia medication (and indeed many other forms of medication), excessive consumption can prevent effective treatment where dementia has been diagnosed.

It is important to stress that *the counsellor's role is not to diagnose*, but rather to work collaboratively with other professionals and non-professionals who are involved in the client's care. Observation is a very valuable tool when working with people who are cognitively impaired and hence may be less able to describe their experiences and feelings. The counsellor may notice signs of confusion, personality change or memory loss before the client becomes aware of it. This may particularly be the case for people who are socially isolated or live alone. If the counsellor has been the first point of contact they may perform a valuable service by tactfully making the client aware of the need for professional medical help. Alternatively, if the counsellor is part of a care plan and has the client's permission they may feed back valuable information to enable other team members to develop a more holistic understanding of the client's condition and needs.

The principle of transmitting information gained from observation may also apply where clients are referred by doctors or medical teams. In some instances clinicians may have had relatively brief contact with a client, and so understandably choose to describe the behaviours they have observed, and perhaps also the results of cognitive tests, rather than drawing definite conclusions in terms of diagnosis. This might for example be the case for clients who have been hospitalised following a drink-related accident, when they are in an unfamiliar environment and may be recovering from both the effects of alcohol and physical trauma. In these instances the counsellor, by the nature of the counselling relationship, can play a further valuable role. People with cognitive impairment show most confusion in unfamiliar situations. Through meeting regularly and in the same place, whether in a work setting or at the client's home, the counsellor has an opportunity to enable the client to become accustomed to their relationship and the circumstances that surround it, and therefore to feel more relaxed. In these circumstances they may feel able to reveal a more developed picture of their feelings, circumstances and ability to cope.

At this point it may be helpful to consider how to assess whether an individual with dementia and an alcohol dependency might benefit from counselling. The following questions will be relevant:

- Is the client able to reach the premises where the counselling will take place? Considerations may be:

  - Can they remember where and when the session will be held?

  - Do they have the confidence to make the journey alone, or if not can they be accompanied?

  - Do they have sufficient mobility to carry out the journey?

  - If the answer to any of these is no an alternative may be to work with the client in their home.

- How much information is the client likely to be able to carry from session to session? People with short term memory loss may display considerable insight into their past life and present circumstances, but as the primary goal of alcohol counselling is behavioural change it is important that they have sufficient memory, or assistance to remember, to be able to implement whatever strategies are agreed in relation to their drinking.

- Do they have carers and family members who are willing to prompt and/or help to implement any agreed care plan? There is a systemic element in almost all alcohol counselling. The possibility of the client implementing successful change is greatly enhanced by the support and co-operation of those close to them. This is particularly the case where there is memory loss.

- Does the client have the emotional and intellectual resources to cope with the potential psychological demands of counselling? It is important to try to evaluate whether it is in the client's best interests to offer counselling. The counsellor must decide whether the client is able to cope with the possibility of opening painful issues, or has the ability to develop sufficient insight for the work to be effective. The decision to proceed or not might be influenced both by the way the client presents at the time of assessment and by information passed by the referrer.

In addition to helping establish whether it is advisable to offer counselling, these factors are significant when trying to decide what outcomes might realistically be hoped for from the counselling work, also what factors need to be in place to make it effective for each individual. The counsellor will also of course be working in accordance with the client's wishes, which may mean aiming for reduction or harm minimisation rather than abstinence. In each case the desired outcome will require a different approach.

Older people with dementia share all the tendencies of older people in general who develop problems with alcohol (see Chapter 1, 'What Distinguishes This Client Group?'), and are clearly particularly vulnerable to the difficulties that accompany problematic drinking. There is increasing recognition of the need for front line workers, including clinicians, to develop skills and methods that enable them to recognise and act upon signs that might indicate alcohol misuse. *The earlier the intervention the better the likely outcome.* Our experience suggests that people with dementia are far more likely to engage successfully in counselling if it is offered at an early stage in the progression of the illness, ideally within the first 18 months. It is also vital for those involved in the client's care to develop a clear strategy of support as early as possible to prevent unnecessary confusion, both to the client and to those offering help and support.

How then can the particular needs of people with dementia and alcohol problems be met to allow them to use counselling effectively?

First, as in all counselling, the work must be genuinely collaborative to be effective. This means that the client must be at least willing to discuss their situation. Counselling cannot be forced. As suggested earlier it also means that others involved in the client's care may have a large part to play in enabling them to participate and benefit from the counselling process. Some or all of the following may help to make the work more effective.

Quantity and accuracy of referral information

The amount and quality of information that is passed to the counsellor at time of referral can vary considerably. This can occur for a variety of reasons, amongst them the following:

- the duration, quality and context of the referrer's contact with the client, and hence the depth of information they are able to offer when referring

- the client's ability to describe information relating to their personal and medical history, as well as the history of their relationship with alcohol (people with dementia are less likely to be able to give accurate information on these matters)

- the client's willingness to offer information to the referrer, and also their willingness for it to be shared with a third party.

In our experience clients who have been diagnosed with dementia rarely self refer, whereas it is not uncommon for older people with full capacity to decide independently that they need help with their drinking and to contact of their own accord. This reflects the greater vulnerability and potential for isolation of those whose alcohol problem is combined with a dementia.

Flexibility regarding boundary agreements

As we have mentioned elsewhere, structure is particularly important for people with alcohol problems: alcohol by its very nature resists boundaries. Therefore it is important to consider what agreements will most serve the client's needs and to be more flexible and creative than is normally the case when working with people with full capacity. Examples might be:

- agreeing to phone to remind before each session

- keeping the same time and day for each session

- varying session length according to the client's ability to concentrate/engage

- negotiating the possibility of sharing some or all of the contents of the session with the client's keyworker, to ensure continuity or to allow them to implement changes that will support the work

- negotiating to allow feedback from carers prior to each session for clients who confabulate (i.e. who fantasise or for other reasons convey a distorted description of their experiences). This may be the only way to gain an accurate picture of what happens between sessions.

Collaboration with other healthcare professionals and carers

Whether or not the counselling is part of a formal care plan, the involvement of others who are concerned with the client's wellbeing can greatly improve the likelihood of a successful outcome. For many people, alcohol is inextricably linked to their daily habits, for example they might drink at certain times of day, alone or with certain people, at home or in a public place, or when involved in activities such as eating or watching television. Clinicians, carers, family members and friends may all offer valuable information regarding a client's activities of daily living, which may in turn throw light upon how they drink and why they drink. Although it would be preferable, it may not be possible to learn such information directly from the client. Others may also help to implement a strategy or treatment plan that has been agreed with a client. Examples of joint working might include:

- substituting activities which do not involve alcohol

- substituting non-alcoholic drinks (very important to find out which ones the client likes)

- being aware of reasoning behind the prescription of medication and supporting it, e.g. teaching skills to manage depression or anxiety when medication for these conditions is being reduced, thereby eliminating potential triggers for drinking

- environmental and behavioural prompts (e.g. remembering to eat regularly can help to keep blood sugar levels more constant, which can improve mood and reduce craving).

Interactive style

When working with people with dementia it can be helpful to adopt a more conversational style and to accept discursiveness and digression, where it occurs, as a natural aspect of the relationship. This tendency, which is often shared to some extent by people with full capacity in the early stages of recovery from alcohol misuse, can also indicate that the client might benefit from help to focus on the matter at hand and sometimes it can be valuable to negotiate this explicitly. Despite such an agreement it is possible that only a small proportion of the session will relate directly to the client's drinking, although often much additional relevant information can be learned within the whole interaction, and any intervention that contributes to the client's wellbeing might also have a beneficial effect on their ability to address their drinking habits. There may also be much repetition, which may indicate matters of particular importance to the client, memory loss notwithstanding, but can also, we believe, be a means of transmitting information which contributes to their sense of identity. To repeat can be to affirm.

Within all of this the counsellor will inevitably be making informal decisions about the client's ability to participate meaningfully. What can be remembered? What is being understood? What interventions would be most helpful in the light of this? As already stated, two other most important questions apply to everyone with an alcohol dependency:

1. What needs underlie the drinking?

2. How might these be met without alcohol?

In contrast to what one might normally expect from a counselling interaction, which would aim to dispel confusion, much of the factual and emotional content of sessions may never be fully clarified. Even so, the act of witnessing and affirming the client's experience is still very important. It is also important to seek or recognise other ways of understanding. People with dementia often convey their sense of understanding through metaphors. For example:

A highly educated Sudanese client with evident short term memory loss soon began to address me as 'my good doctor' conveying, I believe, his understanding that I was someone who was involved in his care and wellbeing, and also his developing sense of trust. I had introduced myself and my role at the beginning of our work together and felt no need to contradict him.

There is also more need to work with implied understanding, because a client with dementia may be less able to describe their feelings and experiences, whether current or past. Despite this, strong feeling can be conveyed through euphemism or even silence, as the following scenario illustrates:

A client in the early stages of a dementia that was thought to be alcohol related was referred following a prolonged stay in hospital. Our meetings often followed a pattern. He would speak amiably and without apparent intensity about practical matters for the first part of the session, and would then become silent for a short period of time, during which his chin would drop to his chest. When this happened I had the sense that he was looking deep within, and a feeling of sadness permeated the room. After a while he would look up and smile as though something had been shared. I never knew what he was thinking at these times; it did not seem appropriate to ask, or even necessary to speculate. However, such moments were clearly meaningful to him, and he later told me that the sessions made him feel peaceful.

Confidence can be drawn, and rapport developed, by finding areas where memory and general cognition are most reliable. For instance:

> A client who attended counselling while under section in hospital was often clearly confused when he arrived at our sessions. Once, after a brief three-way meeting with his keyworker, we began by remembering the names of the football team he supported in his youth, which fortunately I also knew. As well as helping me to learn a little more about his memories and ability to remember, he clearly enjoyed the exercise and it set the tone for the rest of the session. Another client with very little short term memory had travelled the world singing in seven languages and could talk about this part of her life with both clarity and pleasure. Doing this enabled us to move naturally on to talking about the history of her drinking, and also indicated that the best way to approach her current drink problem was via its past effects.

One final point is that, above all, this work can call for pragmatism. Successful outcomes depend on an individual approach and a willingness to try different options, as the following experience illustrates:

> A client whose social life had always revolved around his local pub decided to continue to visit after a seven-month spell in hospital due to drink-related illness. As he was clear that he would be abstinent henceforth the landlord and friends with whom he sat all agreed to offer him only soft drinks, an arrangement with which he was surprisingly comfortable. He felt that the alternative, loneliness and isolation, was more likely to trigger relapse.

For the purposes of this chapter we have chosen not to differentiate between the various types of dementia, although we would advocate that counsellors working in the field of dementia should seek training regarding the differing ways in which each illness may affect the sufferer. As we have mentioned, in our experience it is not uncommon for clients to be referred without a specific diagnosis of dementia or, where there is a diagnosis, for the type of dementia to remain unspecified.

The issue of prior knowledge of diagnosis highlights a potential dilemma facing the counsellor who works with medical teams: although it is valuable to have as much background information as possible, it is also vital to be able to relate to the client as they present in the room. It is therefore important that the counsellor does not make assumptions on the basis of a diagnosis. Although each type of dementia is typically associated with certain characteristics, the client's personality prior to the onset of dementia will influence the individual presentation of the illness, as will many other factors. However, if something of the client's personal history is known, disparities between the client's former and present personality might offer clues to their current issues and challenges. For instance, if a client displays uncharacteristic anger, it might be helpful to explore what changes, and perhaps frustrations, could have triggered it.

It is of course important to be aware that some dementias may change an individual's personality considerably as they progress. The progression and consequences of a dementia can be dynamic and so it is essential to try to be with the client in their current experience. It is also helpful to try to build an overall picture of themes and trends that may be revealed within the counselling relationship. This will help to contextualise and perhaps explain changes in the client's presentation from session to session.

Although diagnosis should not lead to assumption, whenever issues involving serious illness present in counselling it is valuable where possible to be aware of the medical prognosis and any implications it may carry. This is partly to enable the client to make informed choices about what outcomes they might realistically hope for from the counselling, but also to allow the counsellor a realistic sense of the scope of the work. Importantly it will also prevent the counsellor from colluding inadvertently in false expectations. This is one reason why

Wernicke-Korsakoff's Syndrome should be distinguished from other dementias.

WERNICKE-KORSAKOFF'S SYNDROME

The term Wernicke-Korsakoff's Syndrome encompasses two related conditions: Wernicke's encephalopathy and Korsakoff's psychosis. Because the former can lead to the latter these are normally considered to be aspects of a single disease (Thomson 2000) and we have never known a referrer to make a distinction between these phases of the illness. Because it is unusual for a client displaying psychotic symptoms to be referred for counselling it is likely that clients the counsellor encounters will be in the earlier phase, in which the progression of the illness can be arrested or even partially reversed. We have encountered a number of instances where this has been the case.

Alcohol counsellors who work with older people are likely to encounter Wernicke-Korsakoff's Syndrome more frequently than other dementias as it is particularly associated with alcohol misuse. This is because it is caused by a deficiency in thiamine. Problematic drinkers typically neglect to eat well. Even those who maintain a good diet are likely to suffer from poor nutrition because heavy drinking prevents the absorption of vitamins and minerals. Therefore, although alcohol is not the only cause of this dementia, it is the most frequent.

From the point of view of the counsellor who is working with the client to consider desired outcomes, the fact that, if treated early, it is the only dementia whose progression is not inevitable is clearly significant. Thus although it may not be possible for clinicians to predict exactly what effect abstinence from alcohol, the prescription of thiamine and resumption of a good diet might have for someone diagnosed with this condition, it is nevertheless reasonable to hope that these measures may have some permanent beneficial effect (Paparrigopoulos et al. 2010). Clearly this possibility may offer the client an additional incentive when addressing their drink problem.

13

DEPRESSION AND ALCOHOL

'It feels as though someone has turned up gravity.'

In this chapter we will describe typical characteristics and effects of depression. We will also discuss how alcohol misuse and depression can interact in older people. Within this we will explore the differences between long term and reactive depression and explain how each may inter-relate with different types of drinking.

Depression is hard to imagine for those who do not suffer from it. It is qualitatively different from simple unhappiness, although people who are depressed are invariably unhappy. True depression has a number of distinguishing characteristics, perhaps the most salient of which is its global effect on perspective. When severe, it distorts perception and robs the sufferer of hope, vitality, self-esteem and a sense of connection with others. It erodes confidence and motivation, so that even if a way out of depression can be imagined, the depressed person typically feels that they lack the wherewithal to negotiate it.

Depression is very prevalent in problematic drinkers and can both cause and result from an alcohol problem, as people who are depressed are more likely to drink heavily and heavy drinkers are more likely to experience depression, particularly as alcohol can exacerbate an existing low mood. This is because alcohol itself acts as a depressant, especially when consumed excessively. Furthermore, heavy drinking can prevent effective medical treatment of depression, as alcohol mixes adversely with most prescribed medication for depression.

The following are some common characteristics of depression:

- feelings of extreme sadness or emptiness

- feelings of worthlessness or helplessness

- feelings of persistent or inappropriate guilt

- pessimism

- inability to imagine change

- lack of interest and inability to concentrate

- persistent tiredness

- impaired memory

- irritability, restlessness or agitation

- sleeping too much or insomnia

- loss of appetite or compensatory eating

- thoughts of suicide or self-harm.

A depressed person will certainly experience and probably display some combination of these symptoms (Franklin 2010). Depressions can also vary considerably in severity, ranging from those which allow the sufferer to continue to function well in the world, to those that result in what is effectively a paralysis of will. Individual experience of depression can also vary in intensity, quality, frequency and duration, and it is well worth exploring the subtleties of each client's experience, with particular reference to the way it interacts with their use of alcohol.

When I first met Fergal he was 73 and had drunk excessively for 45 years. Misuse of alcohol had affected every area of his life. In addition to his struggle with alcohol he described a long history of depression, for which he took prescribed medication. During the previous year a CBT (cognitive behavioural therapy) psychotherapist had treated him for both his alcohol use and depression. While in treatment he had managed to remain abstinent, but had relapsed when the work ended. His therapist had now referred him to me on the basis that he would need further longer term work. By the time I met him he was once again abstinent and hoping to remain so.

In our first session Fergal was keen to try to define and understand his experience of depression, particularly as he had come to believe it might be better described as anxiety. He said that it occurred mainly upon waking, whether from a night's sleep or from a nap during the day. He also said that it appeared to be triggered by certain foods, and that the depressive or anxious feeling was centred intensely in his stomach. Regarding this a psychiatrist had once told him: 'You don't feel depression in your stomach, you feel it in your head.'

We spent some time exploring his previous experiences of therapy, what had worked and what had not, and I asked what he hoped for from our meetings. Fergal recognised that he had a tendency to digress – he was a natural story teller and lateral thinker – and said that in the past this had prevented him from using therapy as effectively as he would have liked. We agreed that if this happened it would be okay for me to help him focus on the main themes of the work, or on the issues he presented at the beginning of each session. However, I made a mental note to do this gently and sparingly as I sensed that the inclination to be discursive and to make oblique associations was probably an innate aspect of his character, and could prove to be a valuable source of insight as our work progressed.

A naturally reflective man who aspired to a disciplined lifestyle, Fergal had developed a number of strategies to alleviate depression. He called these his 'rituals' and we listed them:

- structured activities such as washing up, tidying and set periods of reading. Fergal felt that these had the benefit of focusing him in the present moment, offering a sense of sequence to the day, and disrupting involuntary and unpleasant streams of thought

- exercise such as walking and swimming, the latter referred to as 'the magic cure'

- designating something to look forward to, for instance a favourite television programme or the promise of finishing work at 6 pm.

He said that all of these helped to 'reduce depression by a percentage'. We revised and augmented this list a number of times during the two years in which we were to meet.

Because of the link he believed existed between eating and depression Fergal took considerable interest in his diet. Following advice from a dietician, he tried to eat regularly but sparingly and at set times during the day, also monitoring the nutritional content of his food. Despite his persistence and success in identifying and eliminating those foods that seemed most likely to lower his mood, the problem persisted.

During the course of our work Fergal returned many times to the themes of depression and anxiety, refining his understanding in terms of their personal effect, and particularly their physiological effect. He was keen to understand the difference between the two terms and to try to define them in the light of his own experience. He found that depression deprived him of hope, motivation and energy, and when he spoke about it his chin would often sink to his chest. Anxiety came in the form of an accumulation of worry that would affect his ability to prioritise and therefore eventually to act. As any form of structured activity could help to alleviate his depression, but not necessarily the underlying anxiety; the effect was often cyclical. At times the two seemed to overlap, leaving him both agitated and despondent.

Learning to understand the causes, effects and experience of his depression and anxiety proved a slow process, but Fergal was tenacious. After almost a year he was able to make a distinction between 'psychological' depression, which he described as 'an exaggeration of mood' and 'physical depression', an intensely visceral sensation in his abdomen. The former followed any period of sleep, but was particularly strong in the morning. To combat this Fergal instigated a programme of early morning swimming during which he used a system of visualisation involving numbers and colours to enhance the clearing effect of exercising in water. Regarding the latter, I was able to introduce him to a medical herbalist, who by good fortune had worked in another capacity for many years in the field of older people's mental health. With her guidance this aspect of his depression eased considerably.

Psychiatrists make a range of distinctions between types of depression as a way of delineating both its causes and manifestations. While thinking in these terms is a necessary and valuable aspect of a medical approach to treatment, the counsellor is primarily concerned with understanding the client's personal perspective on the experience of depression, and depression as it is described in the counselling room can often be many faceted and therefore hard to categorise definitively. It is very important however that the counsellor is able to recognise when a client is in need of medical or psychiatric help. Two clear indicators are:

- current specific suicidal ideation

- high levels of self-neglect that could endanger the client's wellbeing.

In either of these cases it is very important to encourage the client to seek immediate medical help or to ask permission to contact their GP on their behalf. It may also be advisable to give contact details of specialist agencies such as the Samaritans, whose support is all the more valuable because it is available at any time of day or night. Where depression is less severe but persistent, it is also important to encourage the client to speak to their GP in order to discuss ways of managing it. Medication, for instance, can do much to ease the suffering that intrinsically accompanies depression.

Although it is vital to try to understand the client's subjective experience of depression, it is also important to be able to make an objective assessment based upon observation and experience. Depressed clients may struggle to describe how they feel and be far from clear about their current needs. This is partially because depression can have a desensitising effect which tends to decrease self-awareness and may, for example, prevent the client from realising the seriousness of some aspects of their situation. An instance would be a client who accidentally badly burned her torso but did not seek medical help because her physical pain was less than that caused by her depression. This leads to the point that, for some people, depression becomes habituated, a way of life beyond which there seems no other possibility. Those for whom this is the case may struggle to make judgements in relation to matters such as self care and personal safety.

Not all sufferers are desensitised by depression. Some people may be acutely aware of its physical impact, perhaps experiencing extreme tiredness and lethargy or physical aches and pains that seem to have no obvious cause. Indeed for some depression is experienced primarily as a physical phenomenon, and in some cultures it is described exclusively in physical terms (e.g. Parker, Gladstone and Chee 2001). This aspect of depression is sometimes neglected, and can even prevent recognition of the source of the client's problem. For this and other reasons we recommend exploring the client's experience in holistic terms, from the potential influence of their belief systems, to the practicalities of their life circumstances, to the beneficial possibilities represented by sleep, diet and exercise.

It became apparent that two particular issues influenced Fergal's ability to feel safe: the ongoing state of his finances and his relationship with medication for depression. Despite being born into a relatively wealthy family he believed that he had 'learned' the tendency to worry about money from both parents. He also believed that this sort of propensity could be inherited: family legend had provided much information about the character and idiosyncrasies of his ancestors, and interest in his ancestral heritage contributed greatly to his sense of identity and relationship with others.

Through our dialogue we came to understand that concern over money formed part of the basis of both his anxiety and depression, sometimes resulting in a state of mind in which he felt simultaneously agitated and lethargic. When I suggested that we might explore whether he could learn skills to cope with this he said: 'It never occurred to me that you could develop skills in relation to anxiety.' Openness to new possibilities was one of Fergal's greatest strengths and we devoted a part of each of five subsequent sessions to relaxation and breathing exercises. He continued to practise and refine these when alone at home.

Fergal owned a small flat, but had given other inherited property to his children, preferring to live modestly. He linked the desire to be frugal and to avoid waste to his interpretation of Roman Catholic doctrine, a formative influence in his belief system and an ongoing source of deep reflection: 'I regard Catholicism as a philosophy rather than a religion.' He ran a small but successful part-time business buying and selling rare books, but nevertheless lived only slightly above subsistence level.

Fergal's financial situation was clearly the result of choice, as at least one of his children had the means to reciprocate his generosity, and would have been very willing to do so. Fergal chose otherwise, and despite the problems it caused him never gave the impression that his frugality stemmed from a lack of self-worth. Rather it had a monastic quality, perhaps reflecting its spiritual basis, particularly as he sometimes quoted Benedictine philosophy. In consequence the decision to live simply had the virtue of motivating him to continue working, and so connected him with his local community, especially as his shop was in a vibrant market area. It also provided periods of elation when business went well.

With regard to this I had noticed that, despite his diagnosis of depression, there were times when his mood was noticeably elevated, almost to the point of mild euphoria. When this happened his speech and manner would become animated and his sense of humour even more prevalent. When I mentioned that I had noticed this Fergal said that he was aware that he could 'get high' and was sometimes able to ease depression by finding thoughts that encouraged elation. Fergal gave me permission to mention this aspect of his experience in a letter to his GP, as I thought it might be relevant in relation to his prescribed medication, which was subject to ongoing review and a source of disagreement between his GP and psychiatrist.

Fergal's psychiatrist believed that he should stop taking anti-depressant medication, but his GP believed that he would always need it. Fergal however was entirely clear that he feared depression more than alcohol. Thus he realised that depression held a greater threat of relapse than any other factor in his life, because if it became too severe he would drink to try to escape it. Despite this he was keen either to reduce his medication to minimal levels or to stop taking it completely, and had negotiated a gradual programme of reduction with his GP. My role as a counsellor involved monitoring his welfare during this process, offering skills to enable him to cope better with depression and anxiety, helping him to clarify what he hoped to achieve by reducing and why, and, in the above instance, offering his doctor information gained during the counselling process that a short visit to a GP surgery might not reveal.

Fergal saw reducing dependency on medication as a complementary aim to reducing dependency on alcohol, consistent with his desire to combat the principle of dependency in his life. Because he feared depression more than alcohol he regarded medication as 'a form of fire escape', as the knowledge that it was available to alleviate depression also served to alleviate the fear of depression, and hence the threat of relapse. Eventually, for a period of time, he reached the point where he would only use medication in times of extreme need, a strategy that his GP was willing to endorse.

As time went on, the counselling process, and our relationship within it, became an additional factor in Fergal's ability to feel safe. I was aware of this and, when we agreed to end after 18 months, had given him details of a local specialist older persons' counselling service, as he was still troubled by depression. At that point he had been entirely abstinent since our work started and I was optimistic for him. Two months later, however, I received a phone call from a friend who helped him in his shop to say that he had relapsed and was in a bad way. After several hours of phoning I managed to get him admitted to a local hospital as a vulnerable adult, where he underwent medically assisted withdrawal.

Clearly Fergal needed further support, and when he was discharged our work resumed. It transpired that Fergal had not made contact with the counsellor. He had been deterred from doing so by concern over the small fee the service charged. He had also become depressed. Unfortunately he was unable to see his usual GP and a locum had refused to prescribe the anti-depressants he was used to, instead offering an alternative that would not have an immediate effect. Fergal had panicked and returned to the bottle.

I had made two mistakes. First, he had emphasised his fear of depression throughout our work. Despite the fact that his mood had been stable for some time before our ending I should have taken this into account and ensured that further specific support was in place before discharging him. Second, he had made clear his anxiety about money matters, and I should have realised that any fee, however small, could deter him from pursuing help. Therefore I should have talked this through with him before ending.

HOW ALCOHOL AND DEPRESSION INTERACT IN OLDER PEOPLE

Some features of depression and alcohol misuse are prone to coincide. For instance, long term problematic drinking is frequently accompanied by extensive experience of depression. Also, late onset drinking and reactive depression often occur together and become inter-related, being similar in that they both signify a form of response to a specific life event or events.

When depression and alcohol misuse present together it is important to try to establish whether problematic drinking preceded or followed depression. If the alcohol problem came first it is possible that the physiological and psychological effects of heavy consumption may have contributed substantially to the development of the depression, in which case it may be alleviated significantly if the client is able to stop drinking. This is not entirely surprising because, as already mentioned, alcohol itself, when taken in large quantities, acts as a depressant. As well, as we have also suggested elsewhere, people who are not drinking heavily are more likely to be able to process their feelings, which in itself can offer a significant antidote to depression.

If depression came first, however, alcohol may effectively have been used as a form of self-medication to lessen emotional and psychological pain and the client may feel unable to cope with depression in its absence (see also Chapter 6, 'Working with Types and Patterns of Drinking'). Such a fear can prevent a client from ceasing to drink or, if they have stopped, cause them to return to it. Therefore it is important to work with the client until they feel confident that they have sufficient resources including, where necessary, medical support, to cope with depression. Where this is possible it will inevitably lessen their dependence upon alcohol, because the potency of depression as a trigger for drinking will be reduced.

Therefore, as well as exploring the duration of the depression, it is valuable to explore causal factors surrounding its onset, also those which continue to contribute to the client's current experience. The following questions might lead to greater understanding:

- Was the depression originally triggered by a single event or was the onset the result of cumulative circumstances?

- Does it have current triggers or contributory factors?

- Might it be amenable to any form of practical solution? For instance did the client become depressed through loneliness or as a result of untreated physical illness?

- Is it continual or does it come and go? Some people learn to cope better when they realise that their depression typically passes after a certain period of time.

- Does it come at certain times of day, for instance during the night or upon waking? If so is it possible to discover why this might be?

- Is it cyclical or does it correspond to any identifiable pattern?

- Is it typically accompanied by any particular thoughts or fears?

Part of the threat of depression to the sufferer is that it can feel both amorphous and all encompassing. Any success in gaining clearer insight can lessen this feeling.

One further point relates to the distinction that is sometimes made between reactive depression and long term depression. Reactive depression, so prevalent in older people in relation to events such as bereavement, retirement and serious illness, is usually characterised as more amenable to treatment because of its shorter duration. While this is undoubtedly the case for many sufferers, others, with no previous experience of depression, can feel totally overwhelmed by it. True depression has no experiential counterpart, and someone experiencing it relatively late in life may find that they have no immediate resources to deal with the uncharacteristic thoughts and feelings that accompany it. Therefore, because it has no obvious precedent in their lives, they have not had the opportunity to adapt, as much as one can adapt to depression, or to develop the coping skills that long term sufferers sometimes display.

A challenge facing long term sufferers, on the other hand, is the normalisation that often accompanies an extensive experience of depression. Whereas any depression colours the immediate outlook of the person experiencing it, to a long term sufferer the flattening of mood and loss of energy and hope that accompanies depression can seem the only reality and the only possibility for the future. Even more so if the depression is combined with heavy drinking, as both depression and alcohol misuse can induce a sense of inertia, reducing the ability to act or to express or process feelings. Clients who show this profile may benefit from the kick start that detoxification can offer, particularly as it will subsequently allow their GP the opportunity to prescribe appropriate medication in the knowledge that it will not be contra-indicated or made less effective by heavy drinking. Experience suggests that medication can make the process of counselling more accessible to people who have been depressed for a long time, allowing a new opportunity to view their situation, and the future, from a different perspective.

Fergal felt great affinity with the clan of which he was a member by reason of his surname and hence shared, if sometimes distant, ancestry. He attended their meetings, which seemed to be characterised by a mutual warmth and courteous formality. This association formed an adjunct to the often humorous identification he described with the lineage of guile, eccentricity, erudition and astuteness he perceived in his more immediate forebears. These connections, rich with personal history, clearly gave him a firmer sense of his place in the world.

Fergal was divorced but on cordial terms with his wife. He also saw his children regularly, two of whom had families of their own. Shortly after we began to meet Fergal had gained a new granddaughter, an event that enhanced his life considerably. He took a sensitive and perceptive interest in her character and development, carefully recounting the changes he noticed between each visit to see her. A picture he brought showing them beaming at each other while sitting together on a sofa encapsulated their evident delight in each other's company.

Fergal's belief system and religious sensibility also gave him a sense of belonging: that of a person who shares a body of thought, however individually. He clearly valued the possibility of shaping his life through ideas that had been developed through religious, philosophical and historical tradition. Within this he was a free spirit, and would sometimes joke about lapsing into heresy if he suggested anything that might appear too radical.

His freedom of thought also allowed for things new, and after reading a book recommended by a friend he became interested in the practice of mindfulness – maintaining awareness of the present moment – as a way of managing the intrusion of worrying thoughts. As well as any benefit gained the discipline this involved clearly appealed to him. He later refined this practice by incorporating elements of flow, which in the context of our work meant learning to respond more spontaneously to his own needs and those of the situations in which he found himself. Though by his own admission he was not always able to apply these practices successfully his attempt offers an example of how disparate spiritual philosophies can be integrated and applied to therapeutic effect.

Because the principal goal of both mindfulness and flow was increased self-awareness I thought it might be helpful to consider his experience of anxiety and depression in energetic terms. I reflected to him that when depressed his mood was flattened and his body language lethargic, whereas when anxious he appeared more energised. Once again, on the basis of his current understanding, we compiled two lists:

1. Depression affects:

   - hope

   - motivation

   - energy levels ('it can rob me of moral energy').

2. Anxiety:

   - results from accumulated worries

   - makes it hard to prioritise (and therefore act)

   - makes it hard to rest and relax.

I hoped that by examining how he felt in the light of these simple distinctions he would be better able to recognise what mood he was dealing with at any point in time. Any ability he developed to this purpose, by helping to dispel confusion, could only increase his sense of personal security. By now Fergal was reconciled to the likelihood that he would always experience some level of depression.

People who suffer from depression frequently comment upon its isolating effect. They may feel disinclined to seek company through lack of energy, confidence and self-esteem, or even when they do so may feel alone in the presence of others. Social skills can fall away and it is easy for the depressed person to become lonely and self-neglectful. Older people in general are more vulnerable to isolation. Depression and alcohol misuse increase this vulnerability exponentially. A depressed older person, or one who is ashamed that they have come to be reliant upon alcohol, is much less likely to feel able to reach out for social contact, or indeed seek professional help.

By the nature of their role, the counsellor who meets such a person offers a considerable opportunity, as the counselling relationship provides the chance to heal shame, to encourage self care and, through suggestion or referral, to help the client re-establish meaningful connection with others.

As in all effective alcohol counselling there is much value in making practical suggestions, and the timing and need for this type of intervention may be self evident. It is not uncommon for a perplexed client to indicate their confusion by asking simply: 'What should I do?' Even without such an invitation, it is appropriate to offer some straightforward suggestions in relation to how they may manage their depression better and, where appropriate, access other forms of help.

Where depression has resulted in personal neglect it can be particularly helpful to negotiate a fallback position that involves establishing a regime of basic self care. Both alcohol misuse and depression can deplete the incentive to attend to health and wellbeing. It is important to understand that the psychological and physiological effects of depression not only interfere with the ability to function effectively but also decrease confidence in doing so. This can result in feelings of helplessness and bewilderment, which can be exacerbated in some clients by a poignant sense of the former competence they seem to have lost. This is why encouraging the re-introduction of simple measures in relation to rest, diet and exercise (for those who are sufficiently mobile) can have such a powerful effect, particularly as clients with this profile may have lost touch with a sense of their basic needs. The client who, for instance, learns to address the guilt and anxiety that can accompany a hangover or any form of relapse by instigating a programme of rest and recuperation will have made a significant step towards recovery. For more detailed information see the section on physiological needs in Chapter 7, 'Addressing the Problem: Alcohol and the Hierarchy of Needs'.

Where counselling work is long term and complex I have found it valuable to hold regular reviews. This practice encourages clients to learn to adopt as a process the habit of identifying and expressing current needs. It also helps to build and sustain momentum and a sense of collaboration by providing an opportunity to recognise where change has occurred and where further change is needed. During one review Fergal invited me to 'be more directive' in pointing out areas of his behaviour that could beneficially be altered or adapted. Therefore, because we were becoming more familiar, I was able to suggest that his appearance and hygiene often suffered when he was depressed, and that attending to these might improve how he felt about himself. Able to be humorous even at the worst times, he joked that he had once been given £2 by a kindly passer by 'who mistook me for a tramp'. Changes in appearance and self care can say much about the client's internal state and ability to meet the world. The desire to take better care of oneself is a tangible demonstration of self-esteem.

As our work continued Fergal became noticeably more confident in expressing opinions, also less tentative in the way he conceptualised his drinking. He quoted St Thomas Aquinas as saying: 'Evil is an absence of good, where good should be.' Thus he aspired to be proactive in helping others, and sometimes felt diminished when he saw himself as unable to be so. He also felt saddened by his ultimate inability to cope with depression entirely by 'non-chemical means'.

He first became depressed between the ages of 16 and 18, believing in retrospect that this had been brought on by a 'sense of sin' at either missing mass or not concentrating when he attended. Fergal, like a number of his forebears, was dyslexic, and I wondered if this might affect his ability to concentrate: as mentioned earlier we had already identified his difficulty in maintaining focus. To this end, with Fergal's permission, I contacted a friend who specialised in teaching people with dyslexia who advised me that some types of dyslexia could commonly affect concentration. She also said that in Fergal's case one reason for this could be his natural tendency to think tangentially, which she also associated with some types of dyslexia. Thus linear thought, including the ability to sustain attention on the matter in hand, might not come naturally. I was able to convey this information to Fergal as a hypothesis for the inattention that had led to shame and then depression. This possibility seemed to enable him to begin to view it as a family trait, rather than a personal flaw.

One way in which alcohol counselling may differ from typical practice in general counselling is that an exploration of family influences may need to be deferred until a later stage. This may be for a variety of reasons. The client may feel a more urgent need to address the effects of their current situation than to delve into the past. They may also need to establish a very high level of trust in the counselling relationship before considering painful relationships or shameful behaviour. Where memory and cognition have been temporarily compromised by alcohol misuse a period of abstinence may be necessary to enable the client to look back with sufficient clarity and resilience. Late onset drinkers may feel that factors in their childhood and early adulthood are not particularly relevant as they did not seem to precipitate difficulties that manifested much later.

For these reasons it is important to be patient and tentative when exploring the past. People who develop alcohol problems are far more likely to have experienced depression or other mental health problems, physical, psychological or sexual abuse, or some form of trauma or deprivation than the general population. For both clinical and ethical reasons it is advisable to respect reticence and to allow the client to disclose, or not, slowly and in their own time. This approach is far more likely to enable clients to speak about sensitive issues, if they choose to, and hence to allow the counsellor to act as a healing witness to previously hidden and emotive experience, and to explore its contribution to the client's presenting problems.

Towards the end of our work Fergal offered this analogy: 'Working with alcohol and everything that surrounds it is like facing the tiers of an army. You have to face each tier and are not always sure what lies behind.' As ever he said this with humour, but also, I thought, with hope. The military metaphor underlined his desire to be disciplined and systematic in the face of the enemy he now saw alcohol to be. Fergal had become disciplined in a variety of ways: in the importance he attached to arriving on time for his appointments, in his regular exercise habit and carefully apportioned diet, in the care with which he tried to apply any new insight in his day-to-day life. Though still affected by depression he had learned to a significant degree to work with it and to apply himself as best he could to the immediate challenges of his life, in the knowledge that other challenges would follow.

I had been a privileged witness as his belief system evolved in response to his growing understanding of the skills he needed to remain abstinent and to live a fulfilling life. He proved able to benefit from past experience and new ideas. He called upon the discipline learned at a Catholic boarding school to structure his day, recognising structured activity as an antidote both to the chaos of alcohol misuse and to depression and anxiety. He was also very willing to incorporate ideas drawn from modern psychology.

At the time of writing he had completed two years of total abstinence – the longest period in his adult life. He continued to run his business successfully during a recession and was much involved in the affairs of his locality. A young film maker hoped to make a TV documentary about his life.

Some time after our work ended I had a phone conversation with Fergal in which I learned that his parish priest had begun to send parishioners with a drink problem to him for counsel. After 45 years of problem drinking his ability to stay sober had become an inspiration and source of hope to others.

14

BIPOLAR DISORDER
AND ALCOHOL

*'I can't imagine what it's like to be
depressed – unless I'm depressed.'*

*In this chapter we will briefly refer to the different classifications of bipolar
disorder and discuss how this illness may affect the perspective of those
who suffer from it. We will describe how clients with bipolar disorder
may present in the counselling room and how the variations of mood
associated with the condition may influence clients' use of alcohol. We
will also offer suggestions that may enable people with bipolar disorder to
use counselling more effectively.*

Bipolar disorder, until recently known as manic depression, is an
illness characterised by extremes of mood and by fluctuations of mood.
Typically sufferers experience a high mood which when extreme can
become mania or psychosis, and a low mood which when extreme
can become clinical depression. There may also be many gradations
between these extremes, often including spells of more balanced or
normal mood. Moods therefore can vary considerably in severity,
but also in duration and in the extent to which they fluctuate. The
proportion of time in which someone can experience a high mood in
relation to a low mood can also vary greatly.

People who suffer from this illness are five times more likely to
develop an alcohol problem than the general population. In addition
problematic drinking can either complicate or prevent diagnosis,
particularly as excessive use of alcohol in itself tends to induce
instability of mood. Moreover, those who misuse alcohol are less

likely to comply with medication, thereby reducing the effectiveness of this form of treatment (Sonne and Brady 2007).

Like many aspects of mental health the condition can be represented as a spectrum in terms of degree of severity. The fourth edition of the Diagnostic and Statistical Manual of Mental Disorders (DSM-IV) describes three categories of this illness: bipolar 1, bipolar 2 and cyclothymic disorder (American Psychiatric Association (APA) 1994). To these might be added what could be described as sub-clinical mood swings, that is fluctuations in mood which have an appreciable effect on the person experiencing them but are not severe enough to warrant medical treatment. The distinction between each category is the degree to which the illness impairs the sufferer's ability to function.

These classifications can be confusing to those who do not work within a medical model, and clearly it is not within the counsellor's remit to diagnose a mental health condition. Nevertheless, they do give some indication of how the illness can manifest, and of its potential to debilitate the sufferer. A counsellor would not normally expect to work with a client currently experiencing symptoms of psychosis, or any of the more extreme manifestations of bipolar disorder. However, because the presenting moods of people with bipolar disorder are often sporadic and fluctuating, because the illness can be present for some time before it is diagnosed, and because an alcohol problem may disguise underlying mental illness, it is important to be able to recognise signs that indicate the need for medical or psychiatric help. Both severe depression and the more extreme manic states can impair the sufferer's judgement, affect their ability to seek help and make them more vulnerable to self-harm or self-neglect.

PRESENTING CHARACTERISTICS OF PEOPLE WITH BIPOLAR DISORDER

The behaviour and perspective of people with this illness are particularly likely to be driven by their current mood. We have found this also to be a general tendency among people who develop alcohol problems, and where the two combine this propensity can be both exacerbated and reinforced. It would also seem that the very contrast between the extremes of elevated and lowered mood can make the experience of each feel more intense and all encompassing.

For these reasons clients who are currently depressed may struggle to remember times when they have felt otherwise, or to imagine an existence not coloured by depression. People with bipolar disorder are particularly vulnerable to becoming isolated and self-neglectful when depressed and may fail to attend sessions, or notify that they feel unable to. Self-esteem can plummet suddenly, and this may be accompanied by the feeling that they have somehow failed the counsellor, particularly as the condition can make it difficult to sustain relationships in general. For these and other reasons consistency on the part of the counsellor can be particularly valuable for people whose moods fluctuate, especially in the form of demonstrating an unequivocal sense of the client's worth. A practical aspect of such an attitude may be a willingness to assume the onus to maintain contact by letter or phone, bearing in mind that depression can be a potent trigger for drinking and a client who fails to attend may also have relapsed with alcohol.

Another and perhaps rather unexpected feature of depression in bipolar clients is that, when not too severe, it can sometimes offer a window of opportunity, in that the client may be more able to relate and to reflect than when experiencing a manic phase. Depression, although it can distort perception, may also allow a greater sense of groundedness and realism, and hence a greater sense of connection with others and with the practical necessities of life.

Clients who present as manic or 'high' may typically speak rapidly and/or without pausing for long periods. This in itself can present a challenge, as the counsellor may struggle to find an opportunity to comment and may feel more like an audience than a person in relationship with another. If the high is not extreme the client may present as unusually jovial or humorous, or optimistic or full of ideas. They may also seem more charismatic or dominant, and will certainly appear more energetic. In the case of more extreme highs the client may seem agitated, driven and excitable, or ill at ease. Alternatively they may present as elated or euphoric. Sometimes, where this is the case, the session can offer the client a space to release pent up energy and they may grow quieter as it progresses, particularly if the counsellor is able to remain calm and centred. We have also found that some clients are able to respond to guided relaxation techniques as a way of attaining a calmness that enables better communication.

Many people with bipolar disorder display a noticeably cyclical process, with moods altering in a particular rhythm or sequence.

In others there may be no discernible pattern, or one mood may be particularly lasting or prevalent. People with this condition can at times be particularly sensitive and responsive to stimuli in the environment, and encounters or events may trigger an abrupt change in mood. Also, phases of each mood can be complex. For instance a manic phase can be accompanied by exhaustion and depression, which is overridden by the driven quality of the 'high', from which the client may feel they cannot escape. Because of this there can sometimes be a disparity between the client's apparent mood and how they describe themselves as feeling.

When I first met Timothy I was struck by his somewhat theatrical appearance and engaging yet diffident manner. He was 60 years old, lived alone and had no children or family contact. He had been referred to me by a clinical psychologist for counselling in relation to his history of heavy binge drinking. She also felt that he would benefit particularly from relaxation training. His referral notes stated that he had been diagnosed with bipolar disorder and that there was a history of mental illness in his family.

In our first session Timothy told me that he 'found it hard to access a world beyond alcohol'. At that point he was bingeing approximately once a week and his drinking took place mainly in pubs and the homes of friends, all of whom drank heavily and some of whom also used recreational drugs. Spaces between binges were partly dictated by the time it took him to recover, typically about five days. After each binge he would feel ill, guilty, anxious and loath to engage with others. Although he found it hard to give reasons for his drinking ('it could be anything'), he felt that alcohol sometimes helped to lead him out of the spells of isolation and depression that invariably accompanied his recovery.

Although he had been unable to work for many years, Timothy described himself as an artist and attended a local studio for people with mental health problems who wished to paint or sculpt. He had left school when he was 15 with little formal education, but had read voraciously and had developed particular interests in philosophy, spirituality and all forms of the arts. Clearly talented, his use of language was always revealing and original and, unsurprisingly, had a pictorial quality.

It soon became apparent that he found our meetings stimulating, and thought about them a great deal. When feeling high, he would begin by speaking with some urgency and at length about a subject or issue that had been on his mind during the preceding week, which often related to a previous conversation between us. His rapid, pressured speech on these occasions was clearly an aspect of the driven quality of his more elevated moods. Much later he told me that, through self-consciousness, he felt the need to 'perform' in our sessions; to adopt an identity in order to gain the confidence he needed to communicate. Because of this he felt inauthentic: a fraud. I experienced this rather differently, having no sense that he was being artificial, rather that the conscious attempt to stylise his persona was a rather touching aspect of his artistic nature that also stemmed from an uncertain sense of self, deriving in part from the instability of his moods.

Timothy's conversation often blended the personal and the topical, and said much about the way his changing moods affected his perception and his sense of his place in the world. For instance, he once mentioned that he had recently become aware of an alarming acceleration in the general course of global events, then spoke about the relentless nature of repetitive thoughts he experienced when he was high. Through comments like this I began to realise that he might use alcohol to escape any mood that became oppressive.

At this stage I was trying to help him to define what he hoped for from our meetings, and at one point, in response to this, he said: 'I'd like to find a viable detachment.' I felt that this statement so encapsulated a fundamental need that I suggested that we might hold it as a central theme and, mindful of the referrer's recommendation, offered some relaxation training as a tool to help him unhook from the pressure of his own thoughts and his sense of a fast and unrelenting environment. Timothy had a long-held interest in meditation and took to this readily.

As our relationship developed it quickly became apparent that his mood swings had a cyclical quality, although doubtless made more erratic by his bingeing. Despite clearly enjoying some aspects of his high moods he longed for greater balance, and with this in mind we agreed to try to explore the changing phases of his cycle, in the hope that we might understand it better, and perhaps be able to discern some recurring characteristics.

I also learned that there had been much instability in his childhood. His mother, who had been diagnosed with schizophrenia, suffered frequent psychotic episodes, and on one such occasion had exposed herself to him. She later died when he was a teenager, and at some point after this Timothy and his brother came to realise that their father sometimes dressed in her clothes when at home. Timothy felt that these events were formative in the development of his illness, also in his lifelong fascination and guilt in relation to sexuality and mental illness. He also thought that the influence of these experiences had prevented him from sustaining any truly meaningful relationships, and hence had contributed to his recurring sense of isolation and therefore also to his habit of bingeing, which represented, in part, an attempt to escape it.

EXPLORING MOOD PATTERNS

The classifications mentioned earlier in this chapter describe various gradations of the experience of bipolar disorder as a way of offering an objective measure of the presenting severity of the illness. As we have suggested, however, the pattern, duration and experiential quality of moods of people with bipolar disorder can vary greatly from individual to individual. This variation can be affected by a variety of factors, including:

- the underlying personality of the individual

- whether they are taking prescribed medication and if so their individual response to it (also their ability or willingness to comply with their prescription)

- whether they are using alcohol or other mood-altering substances

- whether they are isolated or have supportive contact

- whether the illness makes them prone to self-neglect

- environmental and interpersonal factors and the individual's response to specific events, relationships or other stimuli.

Counsellors working with people with this condition may find it helpful to explore the client's subjective experience of moods and changes in mood in terms of what influence these have upon their thoughts, feelings, behaviour and interaction with others. As a complementary measure it is also valuable to try to form an objective impression of any patterns that become apparent in relation to changes of mood, as these can sometimes be more perceptible to an observer than to the person caught up in them.

People with bipolar disorder often have a noticeably cyclical process, with gradations of highs following gradations of lows in a recognisable sequence and pattern. Within such cycles moods can sometimes be observed to have identifiable characteristics. Changes of mood may also have typical or repetitive triggers. Therefore, when exploring the client's process it may be helpful to consider the following:

- How long do phases of mood tend to last?

- Is there any consistency in lengths of phases?

- Is it possible to identify any triggers for abrupt changes from one phase to another?

- Are they more able to communicate effectively or to express themselves in a particular mood or moods?

- Do they use alcohol, consciously or unconsciously, to alter a mood or moods?

- Is it possible to ascertain whether mood swings or instability of mood preceded problematic drinking?

It is important also to understand that not all people with bipolar disorder will display mood swings or instability with regard to their moods. Some, for instance, undergo extended and intractable periods of depression, which can remain apparently unalleviated by a more elevated mood during the course of even long term counselling. Additionally clients whose condition has been stabilised by medication may display little evidence of appreciable mood swings.

There was often a quality of shamed confession in Timothy's manner, particularly when he was depressed. He struggled to view himself as a person of worth and craved the acceptance of others. I learned that his shame sprung from a variety of sources. The extreme contrasts in his mood cycle led to polarities in his behaviour and these made him feel ashamed, as he believed that his inability to be consistent evidenced a lack of genuineness. This shame was amplified by the background of shame that his family had felt in relation to his mother's illness, made worse still by his shame of having felt ashamed of her. Alongside shame was much fear. Timothy felt terrified of 'becoming like her'. Despite this he longed for the aspect of her condition that, in his perception, allowed her to retreat from the world. He told me, without resentment, that he believed that her periods of psychosis effectively absolved her of responsibility while they were happening.

Reflecting on this, I felt that his current pattern of behaviour did, in a different way, allow him a form of withdrawal, particularly as the indulgence and disinhibition characterised by his description of his binges alternated with periods of asceticism and self-punishment, as he recovered and prepared to face the world again. I wondered whether it might be possible for him to distinguish between a genuine recurring need for respite, both from the associated terror of his mother's psychosis and the apparent implication that something so extreme was necessary to gain permission to retreat into himself. Later, when it felt right, I suggested that at times when things got too intense he perhaps simply needed to rest and be alone, and that this was okay. In saying this I felt a strong need to convey my own overt acceptance both of Timothy as a person and of the dilemmas caused by his illness. This feeling would return many times during the two years in which we met.

Over the next year a major focus of our work involved helping him to develop self-awareness in relation to his changing moods and the effect of alcohol within them. I also gradually began to suggest skills which I hoped would enable him better self-regulation. We continued with occasional sessions of relaxation, and the first significant breakthrough came when he realised at the start of a session that he was too high to engage effectively, and asked to begin with a guided relaxation so that he could centre himself sufficiently in order to be able to converse. At other times, when high and burdened with many thoughts, he would ask for 10 or 15 minutes in which to speak uninterrupted. These bursts of expression seemed to allow him to 'come down', and to become quieter and more receptive. In doing this I believe he was attempting to contain the urgency of needing to release his pent up thoughts within a defined period, a progression in terms of both self-awareness and self-control.

In contrast, when in a calmer mood, Timothy often found our meetings stimulating. Ironically this in itself could provide a trigger for drinking, as an interesting conversation could lift his mood into a pleasant high, which he would then want to prolong and indeed intensify with alcohol. The next major breakthrough was when he realised this as it was happening shortly after a session, and decided to forgo a visit to the pub, instead going home to be quiet. In doing this he demonstrated an understanding that he sometimes used alcohol to sustain a high mood. He also realised that, although the high was initially enjoyable, when inflamed by alcohol it could escalate to such intensity that he would eventually want to drink more to escape it.

HOW ALCOHOL AND BIPOLAR DISORDER INTERACT

Anyone who drinks to problematic levels is more likely to experience mood swings and extremes of mood. This is because alcohol typically has the effect of heightening moods and emotional responses. Consequently it will also tend to exacerbate any existing tendency in those who experience moods such as depression and/or elation, or whose moods tend to be unstable or erratic. For people with bipolar disorder, the effect of alcohol can be particularly treacherous and unpredictable, as it may either reverse a current mood or alternatively amplify or prolong it. In either case, the result is likely to be even greater inability to regulate mood states and behaviour stemming from them. Furthermore, because alcohol tends to make moods more extreme it also tends to make swings between moods more severe. We have already described how alcohol can contribute to or cause depression. It can also increase elation or euphoria and therefore contribute to manic states.

Because of the instability the illness creates, the recurrent feeling or appearance of being out of control is a primary characteristic of people with bipolar disorder. They may typically feel at the mercy of a changing spectrum of powerful moods, each of which dominates their current perspective. This propensity highlights a particular difficulty for those who also drink problematically, as their relationship with alcohol is likely to link intrinsically with their mood states, which act as potent triggers for drinking. Because by the nature of the illness each mood is contrasted by another to which it is antithetical, each presenting mood trigger for drinking may be twinned with a contrary and, to the client, equally valid one which is generated by the opposite mood. Therefore paradoxical (or contradictory) drinking can stem directly from the experience of polarised moods. An example would be a musician who, feeling tired and nervous, drinks before getting on stage to create an adrenalin effect to enhance their energy during performance, but who then feels unable to switch off afterwards and so drinks to relax. For more information on this type of drinking see Chapter 3, 'Reasons for Drinking: Alcohol and Paradox'. See also Figure 14.1 on page 191.

The confusion and suffering that can accompany bipolar disorder clearly creates a powerful temptation to self-medicate with alcohol, and it is not surprising that there is a far greater statistical likelihood that people with this condition will also develop an alcohol problem. Furthermore the presence of alcohol complicates both medical diagnosis and treatment, the former because of the influence of alcohol on mood states and the latter because alcohol both mixes adversely with medications used for the condition and reduces their effectiveness. Also, a sufferer who develops an alcohol problem is less likely to take prescribed medication consistently, thereby further reducing the possibility of effective treatment.

For these reasons the counsellor can play an important role both in helping clients to develop self-awareness and skills in relation to their personal experience of living with bipolar disorder and in understanding motives for drinking and the multiple effects that alcohol can have upon their moods. In addition those who are able to reduce or stop drinking as a result of counselling will have a far greater chance of receiving and benefiting from effective medical treatment.

Counsellors may help clients with a dual diagnosis of bipolar disorder and alcohol misuse in the following ways by:

- encouraging clients who experience mood swings or extreme moods to seek medical assistance, if they have not already done so

- encouraging compliance with medication, or helping clients to drink less or stop drinking, so that medication can have greater effect

- helping clients to recognise where moods and changes in mood might trigger drinking

- helping clients to recognise factors that influence moods

- helping clients to respond to the needs that underlie moods in ways that do not involve alcohol

- where moods have a cyclical pattern, working with clients to identify recognisable phases within their cycle and then to identify triggers for drinking that are associated with these

- helping clients to learn to regulate moods, as far as this is possible, for instance, raising flattened mood through dialogue in therapy or teaching relaxation to reduce the agitation that can accompany highs and therefore to enable better communication

- encouraging better self care and helping clients to develop self-management skills. Regular physical activity, good diet and rest will all help decrease craving for alcohol and may also enable better regulation of moods

- demonstrating acceptance and encouraging self-acceptance, thereby modelling consistency in the face of extreme and confusing internal experience.

Timothy and I carried out a full review of our work together when we had been meeting for just over a year. He began by saying that he now felt more able to 'check in with myself'; to recognise his moods and the things that influenced them. With regard to this I had previously offered him a simple key for self-monitoring, suggesting that he might develop the habit of asking: 'How am I? What do I need? Therefore what do I need to do?' An example of applying this would be the need to become aware of times when he was tired, a condition he described as a 'lethal' trigger for drinking. Asking these questions on a daily basis helped him to notice a build-up of tiredness (not always an easy matter as he could be both high and exhausted at the same time) and respond to it by recognising the need to rest and allowing himself to act upon it.

With regard to his drinking he had made clear progress. Although he was still unable to imagine a life without alcohol his binges had become less frequent, typically with three to four weeks between each. They were also less severe, and the fact that they were shorter in duration meant that he spent less time in recovery and experienced less hangover-related depression. Furthermore, occasions of social drinking were less likely to escalate into binges, a considerable demonstration of control for someone with his history of drinking. The fact that he was drinking less had also allowed his GP to review his medication, with the result that he was prescribed an increased dosage of mood stabilisers, and in consequence felt that his mood swings were less extreme.

Timothy also felt that he had grown less punitive in his self-criticism, finding some consolation with regard to the volatility and complexity of his character. He had come to appreciate that the range of moods he experienced enabled him to empathise with emotional diversity in others, and hence develop a better understanding of human nature. He also believed that his art improved during moderately high moods, as they were usually accompanied by a sense of inspiration. Nevertheless he also recognised that the repeated experience of multiple and transitory moods often caused him to feel fragmented, and he believed that this linked intrinsically with the inauthenticity he felt he displayed towards others. We were able to identify three aspects to this. First, his ever changing feelings had prevented him from developing a unified sense of himself as a person. Second, his moods prevented him from behaving consistently towards others, something he particularly aspired to. Third, he felt that his ready empathy could lead to him being 'filled up and taken over by other people' resulting in a further loss of sense of identity. To illustrate this he gave the example of speaking in different accents to different people – 'I become like the people I'm with'.

Within these dilemmas lay a deep yearning for peace and self-acceptance, perhaps best described by the 'viable detachment' he had hoped for at the beginning of our work. I felt that there was still much to do in trying to help him release the oppressive feelings of guilt and shame regarding his relationship with his parents, amplified by the abandonment he continued to feel in relation to his mother's mental illness and early death. I also felt that it would be helpful, if possible, to develop an even clearer picture of the cyclical effects of his moods, and particularly their influence on his drinking, and based on his descriptions I developed the following diagram to illustrate a typical pattern:

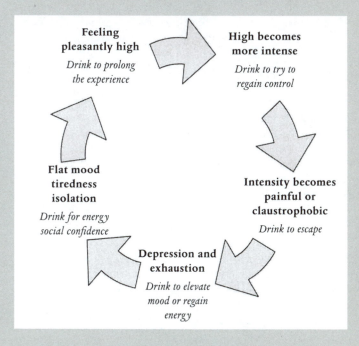

Figure 14.1: An illustration of cyclical process

Timothy had a highly developed visual sense and we had found previously that diagrams and drawings could sometimes make complex issues more accessible. This diagram helped us to work more deeply and accurately with each of the phases he described, as well as defining the way in which they triggered drinking. We returned to it on a number of occasions and sometimes I would ask 'Where do you feel you are now?' As a result he became more able to tune into his current mood and its potential consequences. Thus when a high phase was becoming too intense he could more easily recognise the point at which it would be advisable to retreat from situations that would stimulate him further. Providing he had managed to do this early enough he also found that reading quietly could help him to come down, because of the requirement to focus.

We also explored his depressive phase, which was characterised by a sense of despair and stultification, looking at what might bring relief or encourage movement. Timothy realised that at times he simply needed respite: depression made the world feel overwhelming. On other occasions he would manage to go to the studio where he painted, where the combination of creative activity and the proximity of kindred spirits could prove healing.

Increased awareness of the nature of his moods seemed to allow him greater self-acceptance: 'I'm different at different times – that's me.' He also became more detached, feeling that although his moods could be extreme his reactions to them need not be: 'I don't always have to be either consumed by a situation or withdraw from it entirely.' He was also able to make a link between alcohol and empathy, realising that he might drink to enhance a sense of closeness and understanding with others, or alternatively to break it, and particularly to escape the need to care too much.

After nearly two years we began to consider the end of our work. Timothy felt he had gone as far as he could at that point. His drink problem had eased considerably, but it had not gone away, and he realised that he did not want to stop entirely. He was still inclined to be hard on himself and to accuse himself of moral cowardice and immaturity, yet he felt that I had accepted him as he was, and in our last session defined maturity as 'coming to terms with what is inevitable'. Therein, I felt, lay a viable detachment.

APPENDIX: EXERCISES

EXERCISE 1: MINDFULNESS

Preparation

- Find a quiet place where you are unlikely to be disturbed.

- Initially try to practise at the same time each day.

- Do not practise when you are very hungry or within an hour of having eaten.

- Use the lavatory if you need to before starting.

- Make sure the room is warm enough.

- If you relax in a chair make sure it is comfortable (you should be able to sit reasonably upright and your thighs should be roughly parallel to the ground).

- If you lie on the floor support your head with a small cushion and ensure that your body is straight and that your arms and legs are aligned evenly on each side.

Exercise

- Choose your preferred position.

- Become aware of all parts of the body that are touching the ground/chair – simply observe.

- Allow your mind to wander around your body – how does it feel?

- Is it warm or cool? Tense or relaxed? Tired or energised?

- Are there any parts that particularly draw your attention?

- Simply observe.

- Next become aware of your breath – don't try to change it in any way.

- Is it slow or fast? Even or irregular?

- Are you aware of it low in the chest (above the abdomen) or high (near the sternum)?

- Is there more emphasis on the inhalation or exhalation?

- Simply observe.

Practise this exercise for 5–10 minutes each day and make a note of what you have experienced.

EXERCISE 2: RELAXATION

- Choose your preferred position.

- Once you are comfortable, become aware of all of the parts of the body that are touching the chair/floor.

- Then allow your focus to move to your feet and, letting your attention move gently and smoothly, feel each part of your feet as warm and relaxed.

- If it helps you may think to yourself: 'My toes are warm and relaxed – the soles of my feet are warm and relaxed – my heels are warm and relaxed – my ankles are warm and relaxed' – and so on.

- Continue through each body part – legs, torso, arms, neck and face – until you reach the top of your head.

- Return to any part of your body that is still not completely relaxed if you need to.

- Rest in this position for a little while – observe what it feels like to be really relaxed.

- Continue to practise this relaxation for 15–20 minutes each day.

Note: If initially you find it difficult to focus your mind on each area of the body, try tensing, then relaxing, each part in turn, starting from your feet and working upwards. Note how differently you feel when your muscles are tense and when they are relaxed.

EXERCISE 3: MEDITATION

- Sit upright in a firm chair (preferably one that supports your lower back, holds your thighs parallel to the floor and allows your feet to rest firmly on the floor).

- Rest your hands in your lap with the palms facing upward or, if this is uncomfortable, let your hands rest palms down on your thighs.

- *Without straining*, keep your spine, including your neck, as straight as possible, and let your shoulders and arms hang loosely.

- Allow your stomach and abdomen to relax, and ensure that you are not wearing tight clothing which will restrict your breathing.

- Close your eyes and relax your whole body in sequence, starting with your toes and working towards the top of your head.

- Gently roll your eyes upwards, as though you are looking at a point in the middle of your brow, just above the bridge of your nose (if you find this difficult, open your eyes, slowly look upwards, then gradually close your eyelids again).

- Holding your attention *gently* at this point, become aware of your breathing.

- Gradually let your attention focus at the point where the breath enters and leaves your nostrils, feeling a cool, refreshing sensation as you inhale, and a warm, relaxing sensation as you exhale.

- If your attention falters, or you find that you become distracted by thoughts, simply return your gaze gently to the centre of your brow, and once again become aware of your breathing.

- It can help to count your breaths from 1 to 10, and then begin counting again.

- As your mind begins to grow quiet, allow your attention to leave your breath and relax into the experience of meditation (which might manifest as a sense of peace, a deep silence or a feeling of mental clarity, for instance).

Warning: If, having completed meditation, you find that you feel 'spaced out' or disconnected from the environment, take some deep breaths, do some reasonably vigorous exercise or have a filling meal. Always make sure that you are fully awake before embarking on any other activity.

REFERENCES

American Psychiatric Association (1994) *Diagnostic and Statistical Manual of Mental Health Disorders*, 4th edn. Washington DC: American Psychiatric Association.

Blondell, R.D. (2000) 'Alcohol abuse and self-neglect in the elderly.' *Journal of Elder Abuse and Neglect 11*, 2, 55–75.

Blood Alcohol Information (2010) 'How alcohol affects the brain.' Available at www.bloodalcohol.info/how-alcohol-affects-the-brain.php, accessed on 19 August 2010.

Cade, C.M. and Blundell, G. (1979) *Self-awareness and E.S.R.* London: Audio Ltd.

Department of Health (2008) *Care Programme Approach.* London: Department of Health. Available at www.dh.gov.uk/en/Publicationsandstatistics/Publications/DH_083650, accessed on 19 August 2010.

Department of Health (2009) *Mental Health Act 2007 – Overview.* Available at www.dh.gov.uk/en/Healthcare/Mentalhealth/DH_078743, accessed on 7 November 2010.

Foster, R.K. and Marriott, H.E. (2006) 'Alcohol consumption in the new millennium – weighing up the risks and benefits for our health.' *Nutrition Bulletin 31*, 4, 286–331.

Fox, M. (2008) 'Counselling people with dementia and alcohol problems.' *Journal of Dementia Care 16*, 5, 28–30.

Franklin, D. (2010) *Depression – Information and Treatment.* Psychology Information Online. Available at www.psychologyinfo.com/depression, accessed on 19 August 2010.

Heather, N. and Robertson, I. (1997) *Problem Drinking*, 3rd edn. Oxford: Oxford University Press.

Her Majesty's Stationery Office (HMSO) (2006) *Safeguarding Vulnerable Groups Act 2006 (c.47).* London: HMSO.

Institute of Alcohol Studies (2007a) *Alcohol and the Elderly.* St Ives, Cambs: IAS.

Institute of Alcohol Studies (2007b) *Alcohol and Mental Health.* St Ives, Cambs: IAS.

Jaspers, K. (1963) *General Psychopathology.* Manchester: Manchester University Press.

Kaufman, G. (1993) *The Psychology of Shame.* London: Routledge.

Landolt, H.P. and Gillin, J.C. (2001) 'Sleep abnormalities during abstinence in alcohol-dependent patients: aetiology and management.' *CNS Drugs* 15, 5, 413–425.

Lemonick, M. and Park, A. (2007) 'The science of addiction.' *Time,* 10 September.

Maslow, A.H. (1943) 'A theory of human motivation.' *Psychological Review 50,* 4, 370–396.

Maslow, A.H. (1954) *Motivation and Personality,* 3rd edn. New York: Harper and Row.

Mateen, F.J. and Dorji, C. (2009) 'Health-care worker burnout and the mental health imperative.' *Lancet 374,* 9690, 595–597.

Paparrigopoulos, T., Tzavellas, E., Karaiskos, D., Kouzoupis, A. and Liappas, I. (2010) 'Complete recovery from undertreated Wernicke-Korsakoff Syndrome following aggressive thiamine treatment.' *In Vivo 24,* 2, 231–233.

Parker, G., Gladstone, B.A. and Chee, K.T. (2001) 'Depression in the planet's largest ethnic group: the Chinese.' *American Journal of Psychiatry 158,* 6, 857–864.

Roehrs, T. and Roth, T. (2001) 'Sleep, sleepiness, and alcohol use.' *Alcohol Research & Health 25,* 2, 101–109.

Rogers, C. (1961) *A Therapist's View of Psychotherapy.* London: Constable & Company.

Rogers, C. (1980) *A Way of Being.* Boston, MA: Houghton Mifflin.

Sexton, L. (1999) 'Vicarious traumatisation of counsellors and effects on their workplaces.' *British Journal of Guidance and Counselling 27,* 3, 393–403.

Sonne, S.C. and Brady, K.T. (2007) 'Bipolar disorder and alcoholism.' Available at www.healthyplace.com/addictions/depression-and-addictions/bipolar-disorder-and-alcoholism/menu-id-54, accessed on 19 August 2010.

Thomas, D. (1940) *Portrait of the Artist as a Young Dog.* London: J.M. Dent.

Thomson, A.D. (2000) 'Mechanisms of vitamin deficiency in chronic alcohol misusers and the development of the Wernicke–Korsakoff syndrome.' *Alcohol and Alcoholism 35* (Suppl. 1), 2–7.

INDEX